the charm of charms

the charm of charms by jade albert and ki hackney

ABRAMS, NEW YORK

DEDICATION

From Jade:
To my parents,
Peg of my heart,
my reservoir of strength,
and
Arnold Albert,
my loyal guiding light,
who both made my charmed world rock

From Ki:
To my parents,
Ruth and Ernst Hackney
and my grandparents,
Caroline and Kirk Brodie,
and Marguerite Hackney,
who lovingly and generously introduced me
to the charm of charms

contents

▲ "I wanted a charm bracelet my whole life," says New York fashion designer Deanna Littell. After seeing a bracelet of Jackie Kennedy's in a 1996 Sotheby's catalogue, she decided to put one together for herself. Actually, she already had a few things waiting "in the wings" to be put on it— a gold honor roll key from high school, a Norman Norell Gold Thimble Award from Parsons School of Design, and an old heart charm with her birth-stone. Then, she "went on a quest" to illustrate her family life as well as all the places she had traveled. For example, the articulated fish represents her trip to Bora Bora; the red enamel-and-gold egg commemorates her visit to Russia to see one of her sons; the angel from Provençe refers to the fact that her French husband calls her "my angel."

▶ Page 9: Lucky charms have a prominent place in popular culture, and these marshmallow clovers, hearts, moons, and stars from the much-loved Lucky Charms kids' cereal are no exception. Finding a real four-leaf clover is thought to bring good luck. Clearly the man-made ones are lucky for jewelers since four million four-leaf clover charms, like this one, are reportedly sold yearly in the United States alone.

introduction

The word "charm" is both a noun and a verb. As a noun, a charm, as we know it, is a small ornament that is often attached to a chain or bangle and worn as a bracelet, necklace, earring, or ring. As a verb, "to charm" has various meanings. It may refer to a personal asset—a flirtatiousness, an ability to fascinate, a seductive appeal, a certain grace. But it also means something more complex—a capacity to bewitch, to enchant, to have a magical quality. Which brings us back to the noun: A charm may not be just a decorative bauble; it also may be an amulet or talisman, an object endowed with the power to heal, protect, or bring good fortune. We (Jade Albert, photographer, and Ki Hackney, writer) have brought to this book a great passion for charms. We both have delightful memories of collecting charms and wearing our charm bracelets as young girls. We both have worked in the fashion business for many years and observed that "charms were back." Now was the time to share our passion with charm collectors old and new.

JADE'S STORY: "When I was a little girl, I used to watch the TV program *This Is Your Life*. Every week a personality would be profiled, and then host Ralph Edwards would present him or her with a charm bracelet that had been customized by Marchal Jewelers of Fifth Avenue in New York. "That was the beginning of my fascination with charms, and the stocking of my jewelry box. My parents lovingly cooperated, enriching my collection on special occasions with mementos to keep and cherish. "Charms became my way of celebrating both the past and present, but when I reached my teens, I outgrew my charm phase and moved on to the next trend. Luckily, Mother knew best, saving my discarded charms for the right moment. A few years ago, charms made a comeback, regaining their old allure. Now they are like my photographs—telling the story of my life. "Bingo!!! A super concept for a photography book, a chance to share my passions and express my eclectic style. I delved right into the history of charms, of fashion icons, and of commemorative jewelry. And into the stories of the men and women who have worn them. And then I found Ki to write it!"

KI'S STORY: "Ask a woman about her diamonds, and you'll hear about a marriage, an anniversary, or a beloved ancestor. Inquire after a woman's pearls, and you'll hear about an important birthday, or how pearls are timeless and go with any outfit. But ask about a woman's charms, and you'll learn not about one moment in time, but about a lifetime of memories.

8

"Accessories are one of my passions. After years of writing about clothing and accessories for the fashion press, and particularly after publishing a book about pearls, *People and Pearls: The Magic Endures,* I appreciated the appeal of charms and saw that the time was right for their return to prominence. But those who know me also know that what inspires me more than fashion is people: The chance to hear what passionate charm wearers had to say about their exquisite pieces—and to show the pieces themselves. I, too, had grown up with some serious, bold charm jewelry and keepsake charms. And I wanted to share it all."

WHO LET THE CHARMS OUT? Was it the designers for Louis Vuitton, Chanel, Cartier, Bulgari, Burberry, Dior, Dolce & Gabbana, and Lulu Guinness who, for the last couple of years, have been pinning, hanging, or sewing charms onto anything and everything?

Was it the celebrities of every stripe who show up jangling their charms for all of us to see and hear? Britney Spears reveals a decorative bauble in her navel; actor Matthew Broderick gives his wife, actress Sarah Jessica Parker, a charm bracelet to commemorate the birth of their son; Nicole Kidman wears a charmed t-shirt (designed by Stella McCartney) to endorse Saks Fifth Avenue's Key to the Cure for Cancer.

Was it today's political, social, and economic uncertainties that aroused in us a desire to return to a simpler, more secure time? The fact is, most charm jewelry is personal, autobiographical, and often sentimental—a sort of portable scrapbook of our lives that links us to family members, old friends, and happy memories.

Or was it because charms really do possess magical powers? Some charms emerge out of ancient talismans, others just symbolize plain old good luck. A beautiful "Hand of Fatima" picked up on a trip to Morocco, an evil-eye bracelet, or a laughing Buddha remind us that charms have protected and enchanted people for thousands of years.

It is probably all of the above!

In *The Charm of Charms,* you will find all these elements—the sentimental, the sophisticated, and the magical. Since charms have been around since cavemen wore them, we begin by taking you on a joyride through the centuries. We show you how charms have been used in various eras: from prehistoric times to the Renaissance; from the sentimental Victorian period to the glamorous Twenties, Thirties, and Forties; from the luxe Fifties to today's bling! Since charms tend to fall into subject categories that are popular with everyone—flowers, animals, family heirlooms, souvenirs of trips, good luck motifs, and the "simply gorgeous"—we've focused on these areas in separate sections of the book, explaining their meanings and highlighting special pieces. In our research for this book, we came upon some of the most beautiful and stirring jewelry we had ever seen, and we share these pieces, in photographs, with you here. Putting together this book gave us the opportunity to meet many fascinating charm aficionados, and to learn what made each of their charms so special to them.

From colorful Cracker Jack prizes to one-of-a-kind jewels of inestimable value, charms satisfy on many levels—sensual, emotional, visual, and spiritual. We hope that you will wander through the pages of *The Charm of Charms* as delighted by the stories, as tantalized by the whimsical photographs, and as enchanted by the artistry of charms as we have been.

—JADE ALBERT AND KI HACKNEY

◀ Maggie White, a frequent model of Jade's, loves to play dress-up. Here, she adorns herself with the bracelet that inspired this book, the one Jade's parents started for her. The charms include a Buddha made of jade (of course); a lucky ivory elephant; and, to satisfy her passion for time-pieces, a tiny gold cuckoo clock.

JADE ALBERT

XO HACKNEY

◄ The names of coauthors
Jade Albert and Ki Hackney
are spelled out in 18-karat
gold "alphabet" charms
designed by Pedro Boregaard
and inspired by type used
in old printing presses.

► Ki's bracelet is a classic
1950s-style piece with large
gold charms. Among them are
a disk bearing an adorable
cherub with a ruby halo; a
picture frame with Ki's
initials; a calendar with her
birthday marked on it; and
Ki's particular favorite (she
loves music boxes), a little
music box that plays "Let
Me Call You Sweetheart."

a magical history tour In December 2003, tiny, intricately carved figurines were found in a cave in southwestern Germany. These miniatures, none longer than one inch and made of mammoths' tusks, suggest that 30,000 years ago, people made use of charms. These carvings—a horse head, a duck-like figure, and a creature that appears to be half man, half animal—are the earliest charms in existence, and are remarkably similar to the charms we wear today. The word "charm" originated in the Latin term carmen, meaning "song," which, in turn, relates to the ability to enchant. From prehistoric times to the present, people have worn charms in order to bewitch, whether it was to "fool" an evil spirit, seduce a potential love, or delight a child. One original use of charms and amulets was for protection, and that remains true to this day in many countries. The ancient Egyptians used charms to ward off evil spirits and protect loved ones in the afterlife, and also to enhance fertility and assure prosperity. The Greeks and Romans lent their artistic skill and aesthetic sophistication to their talismans, which resulted in incredibly beautiful works of art that they wore as decorative jewelry. During the Italian Renaissance, in the fifteenth and sixteenth centuries, interest in Greek and Roman art was renewed, and the art of jewelry making benefited. In addition to their use as protective devices and decorative jewels, charms also began to be worn as personal identification. Prominent citizens wore charms to identify their family ancestry, occupation, or political prestige, much the way we use sorority and fraternity pins, school emblems, military medals, or family crests today. From the Renaissance period on, charms were often used by the European aristocracy. Catherine de Médicis (1519–1589), during her tenure as queen of France, wore an amuletic charm bracelet that supposedly possessed occult powers. Queen Elizabeth I of England (1532–1603) is said to have trusted the virtues of a talisman she wore around her neck, a pendant of gold engraved with mystical characters. Queen Victoria of England (1819–1901) imbued charms with sentimentality and romanticism, which, to a great extent, is how we view charms today. She celebrated her devotion to family with a variety of bracelets and pins bedecked with charm miniatures of her husband and children. She even had the pebbles that her husband, Prince Albert, collected for her in her beloved Scotland, set in silver.

▲ This romantic sailboat scene is from a bracelet made by the international jewelers, Van Cleef & Arpels, and epitomizes jewelry of the 1950s.

▶ Queen Victoria understood the symbolic power of jewelry. She owned and wore fabulous jewels, including the historic 108.93-karat Koh-i-Noor diamond, but her personal contribution to jewelry style was her passion for charm bracelets and sentimental trinkets. One bracelet had lockets containing her children's hair together with miniature portraits of each child. Another featured a portrait of her beloved husband, Prince Albert.

By the end of the Victorian era, the use of charms as sentimental baubles was no longer confined to queens and nobles. The Industrial Revolution of the mid-nineteenth century made metal charms available in quantity and at lower prices. Throughout Victorian society, young couples began exchanging diminutive charms: A young man might wear his lady's portrait, edged in pearls, as a watch fob; a young woman might have a diamond-framed photograph of her beau as a locket charm.

The prosperity that followed World War I affected the styles of charm jewelry and the materials and techniques employed to make them, both in Europe and in the United States. The 1920s was a heyday for charm makers, and despite the Depression, jewelry designers of the 1930s also produced impressive pieces. According to Carol Elkins, Vice President of Sotheby's, New York:

"The charm bracelets that attract the most attention among collectors are vintage Art Deco bracelets from the 1920s and 1930s, when charms were made from platinum and set with diamonds and colored stones, and depicted whimsical motifs of everyday life and the heady, urban world of café society." After World War II, when metal was once again readily available, big, gold charms became very fashionable. "In the 1950s, charm bracelets were reaching another peak in popularity, and they were often very sentimental in theme," says Nicholas Luchsinger, Vice-President, the jewelry department of Christie's, New York. "Doris Duke had a charm bracelet of her swimming medals that she wore frequently."

American movie stars like Elizabeth Taylor brought the fashions of the time to fans worldwide, while Hollywood jewelers like Paul Flato and Trabert & Hoeffer-Mauboussin supplied movie stars with jewelry that had star quality all its own. High-profile charm wearers promoted the idea that charm bracelets were linked to one's life and family and were profoundly feminine. Middle-class Americans took up the trend with verve, often turning to less precious metals, like silver, for their charms.

Now in the twenty-first century, charms bewitch us once again! Charm-bedecked bracelets, necklaces, pins, and other adornments are being crafted by couture designers, heralded by fashion editors, and bought by women seeking an accessory that is unique and personal. From sentimental grandmothers to rocker chicks, everyone is joining the fun.

◀ Jade Albert's hairy muse, Albert Albert—her own Prince Albert—has a chic charm collection, gathered while accompanying Jade on her travels to flea markets and antique shops. Like any stylish New Yorker, Albert knows his designers and chooses only the best pieces, such as these three gold charms (a crowned heart, an angel, and a sun disk) by the contemporary jewelry designer Barry Kieselstein-Cord.

▲ This extraordinary bracelet is by jeweler Raymond C. Yard, whose clients from the 1920s to the 1940s included the elite of American society. Today, the bracelet's owner is Elizabeth Woolworth (left), the granddaughter of Pauline Stanbury Woolworth, who was known as "Gaga." Elizabeth received her bracelet as a Christmas gift from her mother in 2003. "I love it because Gaga picked out all of the charms for herself and then gave the bracelet to Mom when she married Dad." Elizabeth's favorite is the mousetrap: The cheese is a heart-shaped ruby—and the trap springs shut if you try to sneak a piece! With Elizabeth is her older sister, Nena Woolworth, who wears a gold bangle set with intricate diamond and gemstone charms from Raymond C. Yard, also a gift from their mother.

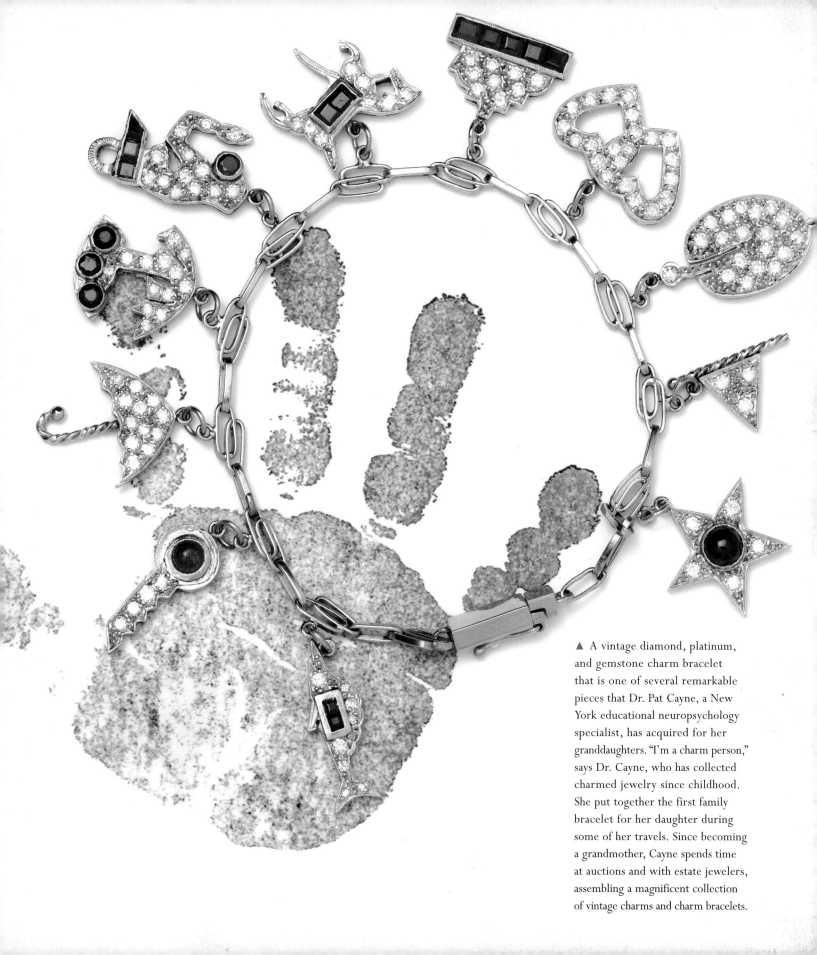

▲ A vintage diamond, platinum, and gemstone charm bracelet that is one of several remarkable pieces that Dr. Pat Cayne, a New York educational neuropsychology specialist, has acquired for her granddaughters. "I'm a charm person," says Dr. Cayne, who has collected charmed jewelry since childhood. She put together the first family bracelet for her daughter during some of her travels. Since becoming a grandmother, Cayne spends time at auctions and with estate jewelers, assembling a magnificent collection of vintage charms and charm bracelets.

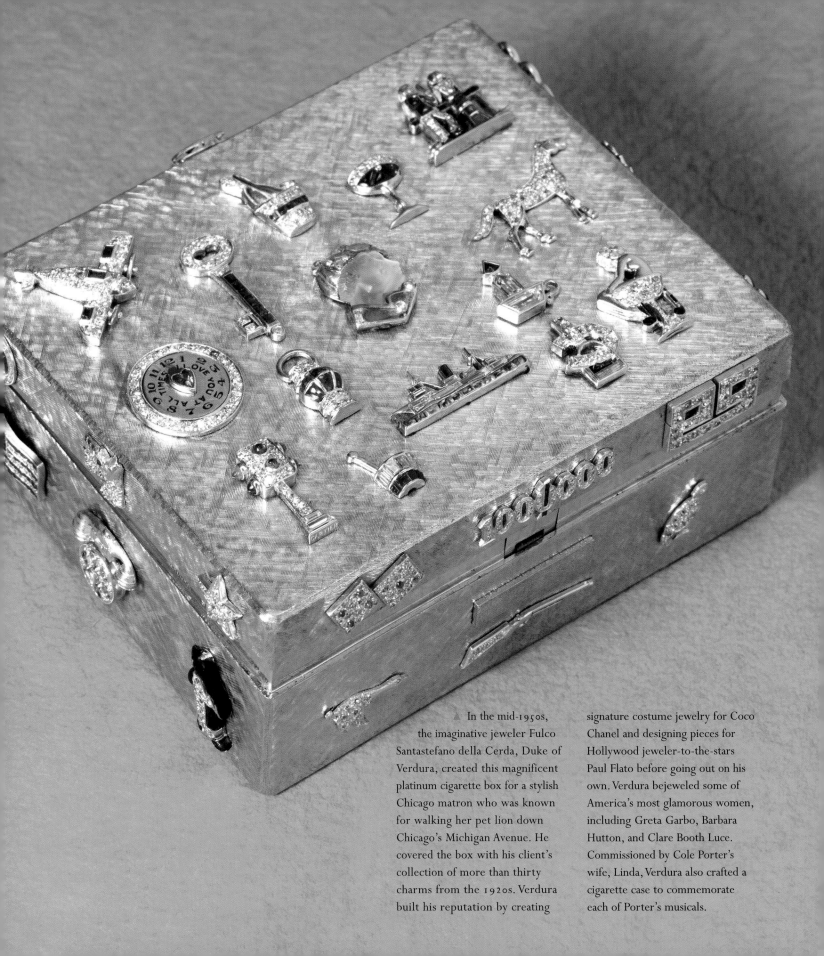

In the mid-1950s, the imaginative jeweler Fulco Santastefano della Cerda, Duke of Verdura, created this magnificent platinum cigarette box for a stylish Chicago matron who was known for walking her pet lion down Chicago's Michigan Avenue. He covered the box with his client's collection of more than thirty charms from the 1920s. Verdura built his reputation by creating signature costume jewelry for Coco Chanel and designing pieces for Hollywood jeweler-to-the-stars Paul Flato before going out on his own. Verdura bejeweled some of America's most glamorous women, including Greta Garbo, Barbara Hutton, and Clare Booth Luce. Commissioned by Cole Porter's wife, Linda, Verdura also crafted a cigarette case to commemorate each of Porter's musicals.

▲ This classic 1950s bracelet from Tiffany includes a heart with a diamond-and-amethyst flower, a Christmas vignette, a horse, a Chinese junk, lovebirds, the "Music Man," and, waiting to be linked, an amethyst clover. In 1945, Tiffany & Co. published its first Blue Book, the prototype for all fine jewelry catalogues, and dainty earlier-style charms, like gold horseshoes, hearts, and four-leaf clovers made their way into its pages. Other early Tiffany charms embraced popular themes such as travel (a passport and an airplane), baby births (a stork, a pram), and hobbies (golf clubs, an ice skate). But in the 1950s, Tiffany designers began creating more elaborate charms that often incorporated intricate tableaux rendered in colored gemstones.

▶ Jewelry designer Elizabeth Locke likes to create charms with neoclassic (particularly Roman) icons and themes, and spends half of each year traveling the world to find stones and antique pieces for her designs. Here, she wears two of her signature charm bracelets. "Each has a little bit of everything I work with," she says, pointing out three Venetian glass intaglios, an ancient Persian seal, and Roman coins.

◀ These charms are made from 18th- and 19th-century Italian micromosaics, and, in the case of the rooster, *pietra dura* stone inlay.

▷ A La Vieille Russie, New York's revered Fifth Avenue antiques shop, specializes in Russian, European, and American art, artifacts, and jewelry. Since the 1950s, the owners have been collecting antique charms from all over the world as family keepsakes. Shown, here, from the never-before-seen assembly: *Top row, left to right:* An 19th-century gold skull charm with ruby eyes that has a working compass embedded it; a 19th-century double-sided enameled jester that features a pull chain to move his articulated limbs; a gold-and enamel box that contains enameled disks representing the four card suits that were used as trump markers for games of whist; a Swiss vinaigrette that features a painted lid depicting a baby in a cradle and contains a doll inside; a gold-and-blue enamel card case that holds tiny "real" cards. *Bottom row, left to right:* A 19th-century porcelain teapot from Germany that echoes the work of Meissen designer J.G. Heroldt; an 18th-century gold-and-rock crystal spinning top; a turquoise-studded gold kaleidoscope from England that really works; a gold-and-enamel sarcophagus from Switzerland that opens to reveal an enamel lining and a female figure that turns.

◀ Large, very 1950s-style charms from C.H.A.R.M. combine the luxuriousness of gold with the purity and innocence of pearls.

▲ This massive gold bracelet belonged to actress Joan Crawford. "Wearing charm bracelets truly was a part of Crawford's personality," says jewelry expert Ralph Esmerian, who owns several of her pieces. "Her bracelets are of a 1940s and 1950s style, and, by looking at the motifs and engraved messages, we know that her charms had emotional meaning for her." Inscribed across the sculpted square links of this bracelet is the message: "Joan, Darling, you are all that woman was meant to be, including . . ." which is completed on the charms: "My love" (on the horseshoe), "My life" (on the genie's lamp), and again, "my Love" (the heart). The crown on the wide-brimmed gold hat opens to reveal a tiny gold sun hat, while the sapphire-eyed poodle perched in a pearl-and-sapphire frame, (made by sought-after Hollywood jeweler William Ruser) is inscribed as if it were a gift from her adored poodle, Cliquot.

amulets, talismans, and good luck charms

The use of charms as ornamental pieces of jewelry is relatively recent. Since the time of the cave dwellers, small objects—often stones carved with symbols or miniature leather sacks holding protective prayers—were worn by both men and women to ward off evil. Even when these amulets began to be viewed as somewhat decorative, they still were considered magical. According to Helena G. Krodel of the Jewelry Information Center in New York, "The first charm bracelets were probably worn by the Babylonians, Assyrians, Hittites, and Persians from about 700 to 400 B.C. Those charms were made of lapis lazuli, rock crystal, and other semiprecious stones and were inscribed with small designs, such as figures of gods, humans, and animals that were closely associated with special powers." Today, the words charm, amulet, and talisman are used interchangeably. "What distinguished an amulet from any ordinary piece of jewelry was its power," writes Arthur S. Gregor in *Amulets, Talismans, and Fetishes*. "An amulet is believed to be charged with a force derived from a supernatural source that protects the possessor." Similarly, a talisman bears mystical symbols engraved on its surface to attract good luck and aid in healing. Many of the associations surrounding amulets and talismans and the powers they allegedly possess have become diluted or lost over time. Most of us do not wear the symbol of a frog to encourage fertility, nor do we crush a valuable peridot into a salve to treat kidney disease. Nonetheless, many of the charms worn today the world over arose from the mystical beliefs and symbols of ancient cultures. Charms believed to possess amuletic or magical power include scarabs, evil eyes, hands, skulls, and angels. Others, like Christian crosses, are not considered magical, but are imbued with reverence and spirituality. Good luck tokens are the most popular form of charms. Today, many of us feel assured of some measure of good fortune in the presence of four-leaf clovers, lucky pennies, wishbones, elephants, or ladybugs. Other classic good luck charms with ancient roots include pigs for prosperity, owls for wisdom, and daisies or roses for luck in love. One of history's most beloved good luck tokens is the four-leaf clover. According to some legends, Eve picked a four-leaf clover in the Garden of Eden. Although the Shamrock, the symbol of Ireland, is a three-leaf clover (representing the Holy Trinity), a four-leaf clover is said to also possess "God's grace." Since ancient times, the leaves of a four-leaf clover have represented hope, faith, love, and luck.

The "Hand of Fatima" has been treasured in Arab and Jewish cultures for thousands of years. It is said to have protective powers and the ability to promote fidelity and patience. This silver Israeli charm from the 1960s shows the typical downward-pointing fingers flanked by two thumbs of equal size. The amulet stems from the legend of Fatima, who, when faced with her husband's new concubine, burned her hand in a pot of hot halvah until her husband, the prophet Ali, rescued her. This charm is paired with a small coral bead, which is believed to provide protection from harm and to help balance one's emotions.

◄ Evil-eye jewelry designed by Lea Seren employs more than 200 versions of the evil-eye icon. Early in her career, Seren broke with tradition by making evil eyes in colors, such as pink, white, orange, red, and green, instead of the traditional blue. "At first no one would touch them, but people decided they liked the colors," says Seren, whose clientele includes Madonna, Kate Spade, Salma Hayek, Jewel, and Sharon Osbourne.

► "I don't want evil spirits anywhere near me," says Faye Wattleton, as a wristful of evil-eye bracelets dance up and down her arm. Best known as president of Planned Parenthood, she now serves as president of the Center for the Advancement of Women. Wattleton has a whole collection of evil-eye bracelets in different sizes and shapes. Felicia Gordon, her daughter, shares her mother's passion for magical jewelry and collects iconic symbols, such as hearts, stars, and crosses.

▲ Heidi Manheimer, President for U.S. Operations at Shiseido Cosmetics America, Ltd., wears nine charm "sculptures" on a black leather cord created by her friend and jewelry designer Kazuko. Japanese-born Kazuko's signature jewelry features crystals and gemstones wrapped in gold wire that she refers to as "healing sculptures." "Because gemstones come from nature, I believe that they possess some of the same positive energy that was present in the Earth at its genesis," explains Kazuko. "I was somewhat skeptical of Kazuko's jewelry at first," says Manheimer. "But I finally purchased a healing pendant and good things started happening."

▲ A deep blue scarab set in gold and encircled by diamonds is worn here by architecture and design writer Suzanne Slesin, who inherited it from her step-grandmother, Helena Rubinstein, one of the doyennes of the American beauty industry. "Madame," as Rubinstein was known, indulged a passion for oversized jewels and wore heaps of charm bracelets at a time.

▼ Many charms are meant to protect the wearer's health or heal an existing ailment. The ancient Egyptians used likenesses of body parts as amulets to protect their wearers, particularly in the afterlife. In Latin America, these replicas are called *milagros* and are usually purchased in churches and offered as talismans to help heal sick or wounded limbs or organs. Sometimes the cast-metal charms depict a whole person or animal in order to represent the wish for a more comprehensive form of healing.

◄ Hand motifs play a significant role in the history of charms. Many hand gestures have outgrown their ancient pasts to become lucky charms, such as the clenched-fist "fig sign" or the ancient "horned hand," both thought to avert the evil eye and other misfortunes. Hand charms often wear jewelry of their own, from jeweled cuffs to gemstone rings. Here, a typical Victorian hand charm set in a fanciful gold cuff clasps the symbols for love, luck, and fertility. Of particular interest is the fish—an ancient symbol of Christianity—and the pomegranate, historically regarded as a fertility symbol because of its abundant seeds.

► This fetching bracelet from C.H.A.R.M. features a number of Asian good luck symbols. The laughing Buddha figures promise wealth, longevity, and good fortune, and rubbing a Buddha's tummy, as one of the charms here invites, is yet another way to ensure good luck. Other lucky talismans on the bracelet include a frog (symbolizing wealth, success, and fertility) and a red lantern (assuring prosperity and happiness). That so many of the charms are carved from green or red jade is also significant, for jade symbolizes love and virtue and is thought to bring its wearer good fortune.

Your incon
will increa
Lucky Numbers 9, 21,

TOUCH ME
FOR LUCK

er than expand business
near future. ☺

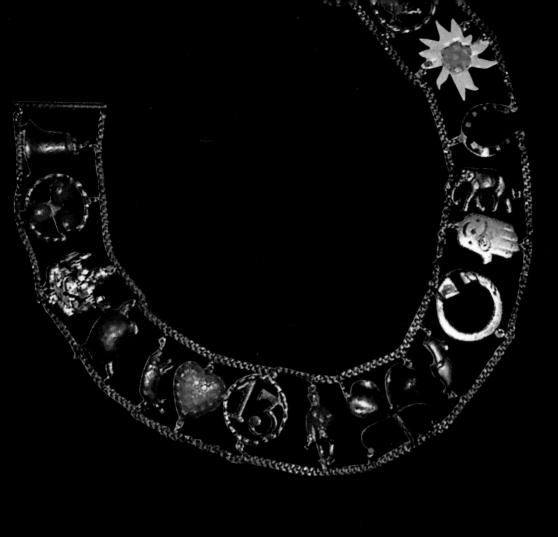

◄ All of the major symbols of good luck are represented in this necklace, a cheeky ode to the proverbial good luck charm designed by Jean Schlumberger for French fashion designer Elsa Schiaparelli. The "13" charm adds a touch of irony—its presence playfully tempts fate and wryly cautions against an overzealous belief in the power of lady luck.

◄ In 1934, when their relationship was still secret, Edward, Prince of Wales, presented a dazzling Cartier cross charm bracelet to his beloved, Wallis Simpson. (Eventually the bracelet had nine charms, each set with sapphires, emeralds, diamonds, amethysts, or a combination of these gems.) Each charm represented a cross the couple bore during their complicated relationship, and each cross is engraved with a symbolic message. The first cross celebrates "WE," the couple's code for Wallis and Edward, while another asks that "God Save the King for Wallis." Wallis wore the bracelet on her wedding day, June 3, 1937, in France. In celebration, they added a cross inscribed: "Our marriage Cross Wallis 3.VI.37 David, slightly imperfect" ("David" was the former king's family name.)

► For thousands of years, bells have appeared in many cultures as talismans to ward off evil and ensure happiness. The Bible makes mention of high priests wearing them on their robes; in Africa, bells are worn on clothing to keep the devil away; in India, bells are put on a husband's turban and around the bride's waist at their wedding to guarantee the couple's happiness. Designer Terry Mayer once strung ready-made bells on necklaces for a fashion show, and soon was making bell jewelry for Bloomingdale's, Tiffany, and Cartier. Now Mayer has over 200 silver bell designs in her collection, and her work is sold in specialty stores around the world.

◄ Eric Ripert, chef of New York's renowned Le Bernardin restaurant, kisses the Caravacco cross he was given as a teenager by a psychic friend to protect him from physical aggression. "I didn't really believe it would work, so I wore it a few times, then put it away. Later, when I was eighteen, two guys attacked me in the Paris subway. The next time I went home, the friend who gave me the cross came to visit. She knew about the assault, and she also knew—intuitively— that I hadn't been wearing the cross. That was it: I put on my cross and have never taken it off."

► What could be luckier than a bracelet strung with tools of the gambler's trade, like these on a vintage bracelet from C.H.A.R.M.: A great hand of cards, roulette wheels, a couple of "mad money" charms, and several pairs of dice. As one old adage goes: "Carry dice in your pocketbook, and you will always have money." Perhaps the same holds true for wearing them on your wrist.

sweet hearts The most treasured trinkets on any charm bracelet usually invoke love or passion, and the most popular symbol to convey affection is, of course, the heart. No other motif more eloquently expresses the most special of human emotions. ♡ Signifying passion, unity, devotion, and, of course, love, the heart shape as we recognize it today can be traced to the ancient Egyptians, who would bury their dead with tiny reproductions of the human heart to act as decoys to evil spirits who conspired to seize the souls of the departed. The heart is also considered the guardian of our innermost feelings, the most vital and emotionally vulnerable anatomical organ we possess. Scientists have found that being in love provokes a physiological reaction in the heart, offering a scientific basis for the inextricable link between the heart shape and strong affection. 🌹 Hearts first found their place in fine jewelry in the late fourteenth and fifteenth centuries, when it became fashionable for European aristocrats to give heart-shaped brooches as tokens of love. The amorous Henry VIII is rumored to have had a reserve of thirty-nine heart-shaped pendants and brooches. Heart-shaped lockets and charms would come into vogue later, especially among Victorian lovers, who communicated their emotions with elaborate symbolic codes, such as the "language of flowers," and who were fond of valentines and poetry. The first Tiffany & Co. chain-link bracelet with a heart pendant charm debuted at the Paris Exposition in 1889, and today the store's signature charm is the heart tag. 🕊 Heart-shaped charms are just as symbolic and, in some ways, even more popular today than ever. Why? Because a tiny heart charm remains the simplest and purest way to say "I love you." ♡

▲ Like sweet candies, this necklace by Chanel, with colorful, three-dimensional, glass hearts is a perfect "sweet heart" bauble.

◄ Possibly the oddest lovebirds that ever cooed, Popeye and Olive Oyl have been with us for more than 75 years. Actually, Olive Oyl debuted officially in 1919, but after Popeye was introduced in 1929, their love blossomed. The two spawned a marketing bonanza as Popeye's weather-beaten mug and Olive's curveless figure graced everything from toy boats to puzzles. Today, these kooky metal figures, with articulated limbs, remain a hot commodity in flea markets and antique shops.

► Love came rushing in at a New York City antiques fair, when fashion designer Deanna Littell was inspired by a wedding-themed charm bracelet (center) that she purchased on the spot. An avid collector, Littell ended up with three bridal-themed bracelets and a new business styling engagement and wedding charm bracelets. Littell has found many wedding-themed charms on her treasure hunts. The Victorian tradition of using "cake pulls," still practiced in the South, has made cake-pull charms the most abundant variety. In this tradition, a number of small silver charms are each attached to a ribbon and baked into the wedding cake or a cake for the bridesmaids' luncheon. Upon presentation of the cake, each bridesmaid pulls out a charm that tells her fortune.

◄ In 2000, Ellen Levine, editor-in-chief of *Good Housekeeping* magazine, decided to give herself a new heart. "It was the first piece of fine jewelry that I actually bought for myself," says Levine about her gold filigree heart and chain. On returning to her office, she found she had lost her heart. "It wasn't terribly expensive and wasn't much bigger than a penny, but I just loved it." Levine retraced her steps, and saw something shining in the gutter. "It was my heart, resting just on the edge of an open grate. It had been run over and had to go to the heart hospital in England—a jewelry repairer—to be plumped up." Eight months later, Levine got back her charm, a broken heart mended.

► Erickson Beamon's jewelry designs appeal to a diverse group of recording artists including Madonna, Patti LaBelle, Barbra Streisand, Cher, Courtney Love, Eve, and Whitney Houston. R&B queen Mary J. Blige wore this Erickson Beamon 24-karat gold plate charm bracelet while performing on the *Today* show in August 2003. The bracelet, bedecked with filigree hearts, seems to echo her lyrics: "We don't need no haters, just try to love one another. . . ."

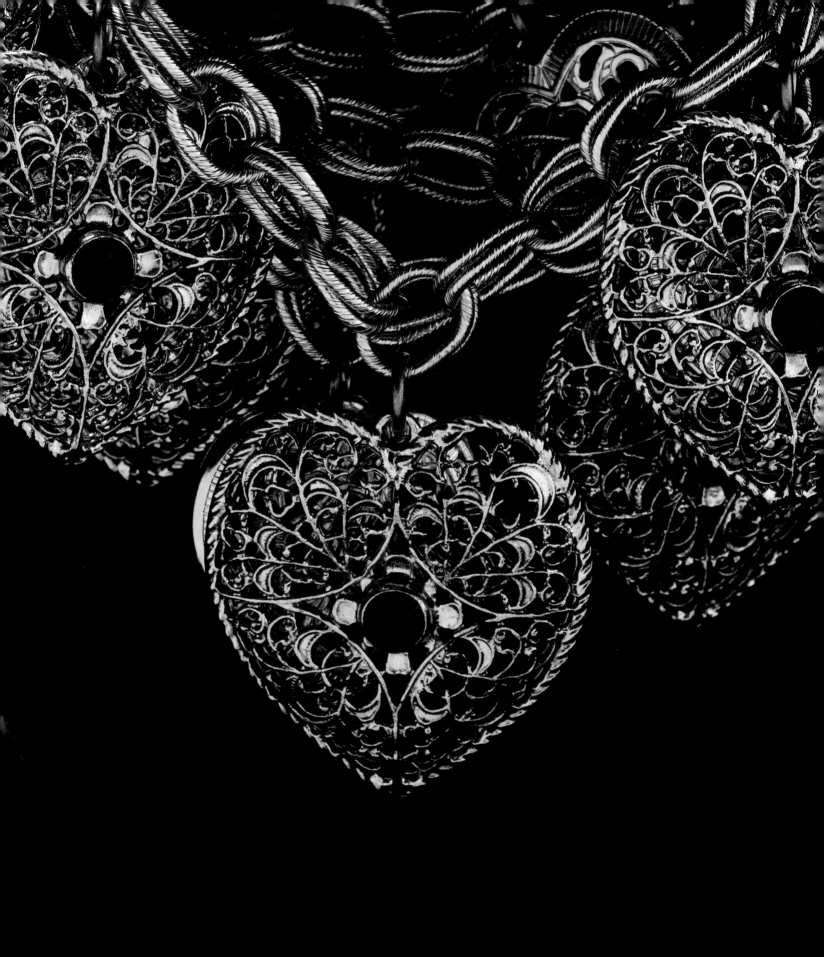

▲ "My mother always used to ask me: 'Why reach for the moon when you have the stars?'" says coauthor, Jade Albert, noting that the line was probably from the 1940s Bette Davis film *Now, Voyager.* Every time her mother reaches for her keys, she has her own bit of heaven to help her, with these dainty charms. Beneath the key chain is a wedding portrait of Jade's parents.

A heart of hearts, all from C.H.A.R.M.'s collection of vintage charms, spotlights pieces from the 1950s.

◄ In a seductive pairing by Harry Winston, each of the major diamond shapes is represented in the nine flawless diamond solitaire charms arranged in half-inch increments along the length of this six-and-one-half-inch platinum bracelet. Who wouldn't see this as an exciting alternative to an engagement ring?

► Elsa Peretti joined the Tiffany empire in 1974, and her designs are among the store's most sought-after and recognizable baubles. According to John Loring, Tiffany's Design Director, Peretti's jewels "are the bestselling designs in the history of jewelry." This sterling silver charm bracelet, first introduced in 1995, combines the most classic and beloved of Peretti's modern, yet approachable, look—the iconic heart; the bean, to symbolize creation; the teardrop, a symbol of emotion; the starfish, a nod to Peretti's fondness for objects from the sea; and the "eternal circle" to embody the never-ending cycle of life.

▲ Cartier's rose gold heart displays two rolling balls, one made of white gold, the other of sapphire glass. The labyrinth, a universal symbol dating back more than 4,000 years, is said to represent the soul's pilgrimage. Here, the two balls represent two lovers who will find their way through the labyrinth, on two separate journeys, converging at the center.

▲ The heart in Henry Dankner & Sons' vintage basket charm actually beats in the same rhythm as a human heart. Trailblazing cardiovascular surgeon Dr. Michael DeBakey was so charmed by this masterwork of miniaturization that he bought three of them. (Other versions of the exquisite basket include one made for the late actress Mary Martin, which features a Peter Pan motif.)

▶ These 1950s copper sweetheart charms, from Odds & Ads Vintage Collectibles, are very Lucy and Desi.

flora and fauna Have a soft spot for animals? Are there creatures that you might like to tether to your wrist, like an icon of your childhood pet? Want your favorite blooms within reach to remind you of some special occasion? How about a bounty of diminutive seashells to remind you of summers at the beach? The love of animal charms began in prehistoric times, and was based on the belief that by wearing certain animal motifs, a creature's strengths could be transferred to humans. For example, the rabbit's skill at reproducing made the animal an apt symbol for attracting for abundance or fertility; and, because rabbits are born with their eyes open, they were thought to thwart the evil eye. Today, animal charms are often given for their symbolic value: An owl (for wisdom) to a college grad, a ladybug (for good luck) to a friend embarking on a new adventure, or an Egyptian cat simply to commemorate a trip down the Nile. Flowers, fruit, and other plant life have also inspired beautiful charms. Plants long served as ingredients in magical potions, and many still have symbolic importance. For example, a pineapple has long represented hospitality; a red rose denotes love, a daisy expresses innocence, and a four-leaf clover means good fortune. Whatever the occasion or meaning, charms from nature always evoke special feelings.

▲ This charm bracelet by New York jeweler Mish Tworkowski, who clearly has a gold thumb, was originally conceived as an ode to the historic Phipps estate, Old Westbury Gardens, on Long Island, New York. The bracelet's clasp is shaped like a potted tulip, and 18-karat gold gardening tools, from a watering can and a wide-brimmed hat to an engraved seed packet, shine like golden fruit on a verdant topiary.

◀ To be bee-witched is to be charmed. Bees are universally thought to be wise and industrious, and are considered lucky because they are said to have come from paradise.

▶ Accessorizing a sundress of her own design, fashion designer Shoshanna Lonstein Gruss is shown wearing two classic seashell-and-coral bracelets by Trianon at Seaman Schepps that were gifts from her parents. "These are perfect, because I love shells and beachcombing," she explains. Gruss has had charms since childhood and fondly remembers a particular gumball machine version with small, colored faux stones in it. "Charms are miniatures—like little doll house furniture—except that you get to play with them when you are older."

▶ The snake is charmed by a bracelet, replete with exquisite flowers and animals: A frog's head; a hummingbird made of glass, enamel, and crystals; a red-and-green cloisonné turtle; and a large fish with an iridescent, frosted-crystal tail and turquoise-and-tangerine-hued scales. The charms were created by the hip jewelry design firm Erickson Beamon, which is headed by Michigan natives Karen Erickson, Erick Erickson, and Vicki Sarge.

▶ Devotees of Marni clothing and accessories, by fashion designer Consuelo Castiglioni, love the spontaneous quality of her creations. On this bracelet, tiny gold charms are sprinkled among three brightly colored Gerbera daisies, recalling the "flower child" blossoms of the 1960s.

► Jewelry designer Laura Rose's mother assembled this enchanting animal parade pin from her enormous collection of charms. "Mother was six feet tall and needed majestic pieces," Rose explains. "I especially like the way the snake winds around the staff, his head peeking through the wreath."

► Laura Love Rose turned to nature when looking for motifs for her first jewelry designs to sell in her shop, Field & Rose, in Providence, Rhode Island. Here is her 18-karat gold valentine to trees (from the top): the trembling aspen leaf with its seed pod, a sycamore and seedling; an oak leaf and acorn; a maple leaf with its spinner; and a beech leaf and nut.

◀ This little dog is heading for home, carrying his vintage doghouse and doggie bowl. The charms are from Odds & Ads Vintage Collectibles.

▶ When Links of London's creative director, Annoushka Ducas, and her husband, company chairman John Ayton, were driving through France on a family holiday, they asked their four children to think up names for animals. Their car game not only engendered Diana Duck, Henry Hippo, Gina Giraffe, Eric Elephant, Chris Camel, and Percy Pig, but also inspired this sterling silver Noah's Ark charm bracelet. The Links of London's New York shop in fashionable SoHo now has a "charm bar."

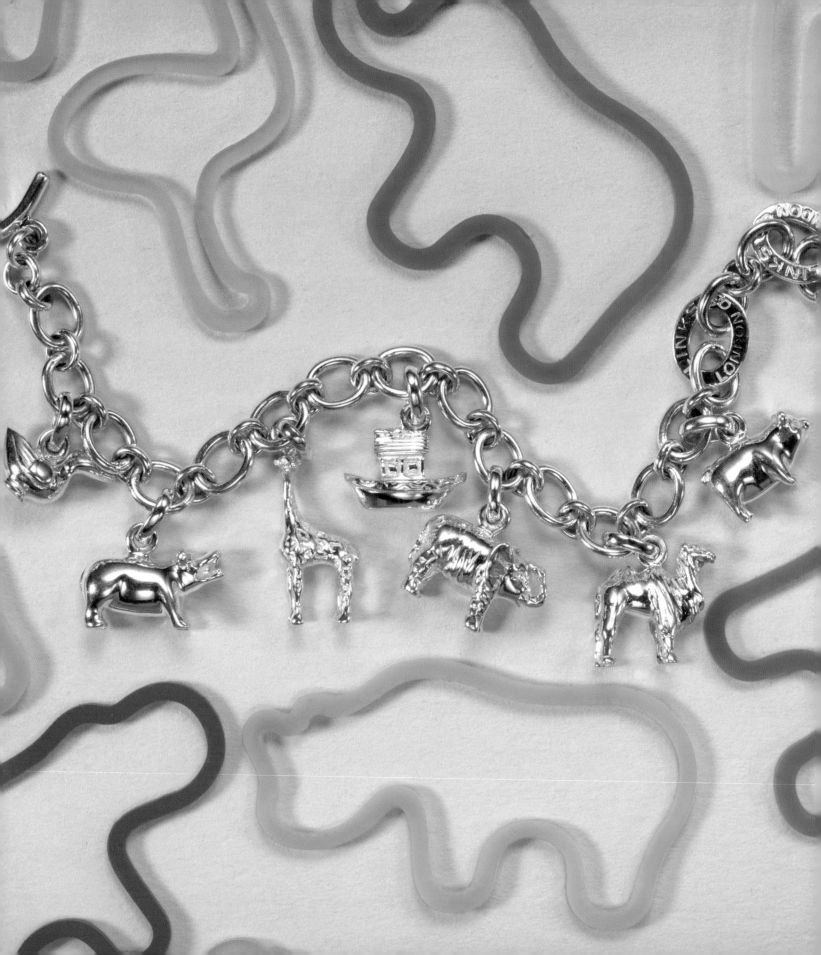

◄ "Charm bracelets are a cross between a power amulet and a security blanket," says Mish Tworkowski, the bow-tied jeweler whose whimsical neckwear, colorful shirts, and rainbow of sport jackets placed him on the International Best Dressed List in 2002. Mish's town house boutique in New York is a mecca for the Upper East Side social set and celebrities, including Oprah Winfrey, Evelyn Lauder, Susan Sarandon, Demi Moore, and the late Princess Diana. Here, Mish monkeys around with his personal good luck charm—a whimsical sterling silver monkey swinging on a key chain. "I was inspired to make my key chain and monkey cuff links for the shop when I was reading about Palm Beach architect Addison Meisner," he says. "The idea that he always kept pet monkeys caught my attention, and I decided that I could have monkeys of my own."

▶ Though Mish is known for timeless and flattering jewelry designs, including his delicious multistrand necklaces of gemstones, such as aquamarine, citrine, and lustrous pearls, he occasionally creates a charm bracelet. The Cabana Coral Collection was born in Spring 2003, and fans scooped up his carved coral, gold, and diamond seashell-and-starfish bracelets. It was so successful that he repeated the style in tiger's eye with brown diamonds. He also stretched the coral charm bracelet into this magnificent coral charm necklace.

◀ Albert's cache of charms ranges from a Victorian locket to a miniature doggy driver's license. Here, dangling from his orange collar: A leather Yorkie, a gift from Four Paws Club pet supplies in New York; a vintage silver locket (a souvenir of a trip to Switzerland, holding a picture of his canine girlfriend, Yorkie Tiger Lily); an enameled butterfly from Calypso clothing boutique (clothing for people, that is) in East Hampton; and, serendipitously, a silver dog bone from a vintage store on Block Island that bears Albert's name.

▼ "My husband started this bracelet right after we were married, in honor of our beloved pets," says jewelry designer Elizabeth Locke. Each charm was selected both for style and as a reminder of Frou Frou, Peg Ear, and any number of animals the Lockes raised on their farm in Virginia. The photo is of Franc, the first of many great danes.

all in the family

Like pearl necklaces and family silver, charms commonly become family heirlooms, handed down over generations. "The instinct to collect charms and pass them through a family is psychologically healthy," says New York psychotherapist Stephen Wilson. "Some societies pass tradition on through oral histories. Some use a combination of things. Charms are tangible conserves; they represent permanence and memories. Because each charm represents a story, they have a richness that no other jewelry has." How these stories are captured in charms is as varied as the charms themselves. The collection on a bracelet may highlight part of one person's life or it may tell the tale of several generations. In the case of a royal family, charms in the form of state medals may even trace an entire lineage. Whether the charms are traditional or modern, charm jewelry becomes a traveling storybook that invites sharing. The rituals surrounding the way a bracelet evolves and is passed down are another link between charms and family traditions. Some charm jewelry is passed down intact, symbolizing one segment of history, such as one woman's life. Other pieces, in contrast, represent an overlapping continuum in which each generation adds new charms to accompany those of its ancestors. Gifts of charms given among family members help relate one's biography, often starting at birth. Silhouettes of children, engraved with names and birth dates, remain one of the most popular charms of all time. Other occasions commemorated with charms include birthdays, graduations, marriages, and anniversaries. Themed charms develop a family tale by celebrating shared experiences, travels, sports, hobbies, and other personal interests. Elizabeth Taylor expresses an essential truth about charms and the bracelets that have evolved throughout her life when she says, "My charm collection began when I was a child, and for my birthday and Christmas people would send me charms as celebratory gifts. As I grew older, they became more sentimental and personal. Each charm has its own story and a particular meaning known only to me and to the giver and brings back a memory and a smile in my heart." Although most charms are meant for women, men sometimes pick up on the family charm trend. Today, a man may wear a few on a necklace or hang a single charm on an earring, as Elton John does. In earlier decades, male-themed charms decorated small jewelry boxes. When pocket watches were popular, charms also decorated watch chains. Watch fobs were another kind of charm; they were made for men but were adopted by women who discovered that fobs made beautiful additions to their bracelets.

◀ Many designers and manufacturers say that for many women, charm bracelets start when the first baby is born. New York jeweler Mish Tworkowski made one or two custom baby charm bracelets that served as prototypes for the 14-karat baby bracelet that Mish keeps ready to customize for each new child. The bracelets here, draped over the alphabet blocks, include a baby carriage, a car with wheels that move, and several animal motifs that are particular favorites from Mish's own storehouse of childhood memories.

◄ Cricket Burns, the style director at *Quest* magazine, and her family boast five generations of charm bracelets. "When girls are born, christened, or celebrate their first birthdays, each receives a charm," says Burns. "Eventually each mother hands hers down through the generations." Here, Burns' daughters—India Tully Burns (left) and Manzi Valentine Burns—are wearing the entire family stash. "When my great-grandmother came to the United States from Italy, her gold bracelet had three or four charms on it, including a violin, and a charm of Brunelleschi's cupola from the Duomo in Florence," explains Burns about the bracelet that started the family tradition. "Later the bracelet included an airplane charm representing my grandparents' first trip on a plane, and a clown charm that reminds me of my grandfather— a banjo virtuoso who loved to perform. My own bracelet has a chalice from my first Communion. It's wonderful to know that charm bracelets always come back in style."

▶ Debbie Loeffler holds the charm bracelet that her sister, Karen, received as a gift from their paternal grandmother. Karen kept the original charms and added her own. Alongside her grandmother's charms, Karen hung a cash register with a working drawer and a sign that reads "heart 4 sale," a beach chair because she loved the sun, a piano because she played, a horse because she rode, and two cats. "Karen was hysterically materialistic," Debbie says. "She thought it was so funny that she found a mink coat charm; it was so her." Today, Debbie and her mother and aunt take turns wearing Karen's bracelet, which is a bittersweet reminder of the vital woman who perished in the World Trade Center on September 11, 2001. On Debbie's wrist is the bracelet a boyfriend gave her for her twenty-eighth birthday. "We traveled a lot, and the bracelet reflects that. There's an elephant from Thailand, dice from Las Vegas, a mermaid charm because I am Danish, and a pagoda because I lived in Japan for a year."

▲ Jewelry designer Elizabeth Locke says she has her mother and her mother's charm bracelet to thank for her career. Elizabeth's mother, the former fashion editor Edie Locke, created a bracelet chock-full of twenty-nine charms, including a tooth, a tambourine, a tea service, a riding crop, and a hookah. "I loved it, because it was so heavy and made so much noise," says Locke. "I remember when she bought the chain in Beirut; and I think the knight in armor was the first charm. But when Mother no longer wore it, I asked several times if I could borrow it, and she always said, 'Absolutely not.' So my response was, 'Well, fine. I'll make my own.'"

◄ Writer, editor, art critic, and cokeeper of the Best Dressed List, Amy Fine Collins inherited her grandmother's charm bracelet, which was dedicated to her grandchildren. "I am the heart-and-pearl charm," she says. "As a child, it was special to see myself memorialized on this golden jewel. I often wondered why my grandmother would ever want to wear her other charm bracelets when she could always wear the one with all of us on it." Collins is seen here with her daughter, Flora, who is building her own memories with charm bracelets. At age ten, she has two: One with puffy silver hearts she received from Collins' friend and Tiffany vice-president Robert Rufino; the other has an assortment of evil-eye charms combined with charms of a camera, high heels, and Paris handbags.

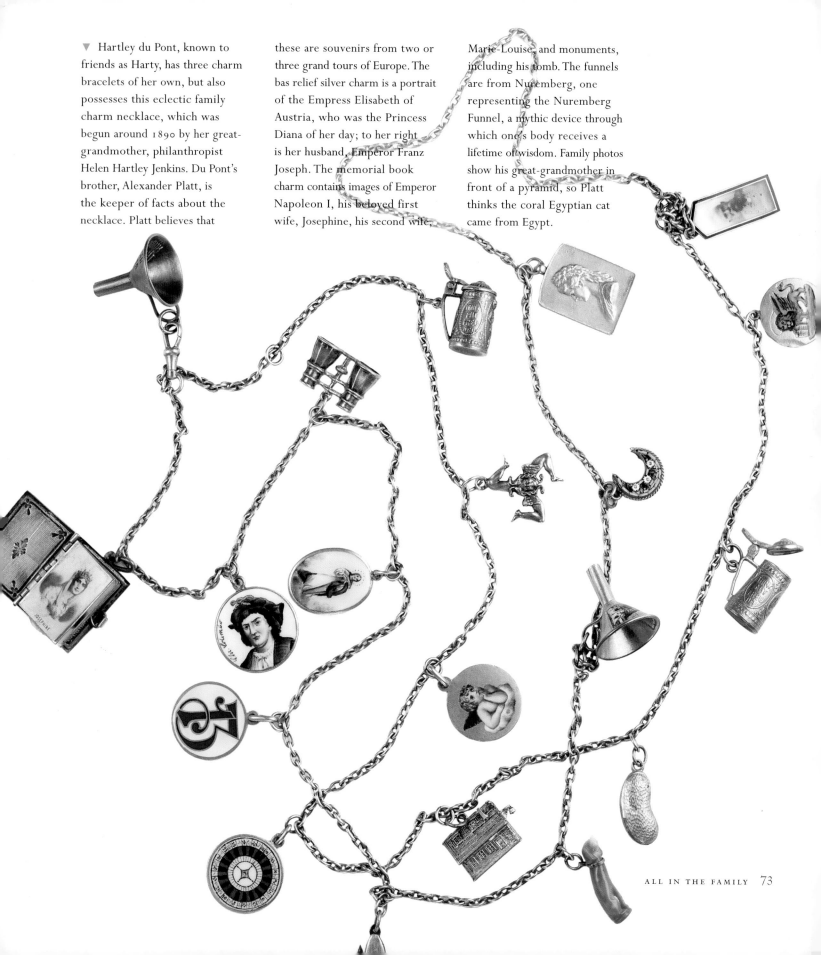

▼ Hartley du Pont, known to friends as Harty, has three charm bracelets of her own, but also possesses this eclectic family charm necklace, which was begun around 1890 by her great-grandmother, philanthropist Helen Hartley Jenkins. Du Pont's brother, Alexander Platt, is the keeper of facts about the necklace. Platt believes that these are souvenirs from two or three grand tours of Europe. The bas relief silver charm is a portrait of the Empress Elisabeth of Austria, who was the Princess Diana of her day; to her right is her husband, Emperor Franz Joseph. The memorial book charm contains images of Emperor Napoleon I, his beloved first wife, Josephine, his second wife, Marie-Louise, and monuments, including his tomb. The funnels are from Nuremberg, one representing the Nuremberg Funnel, a mythic device through which one's body receives a lifetime of wisdom. Family photos show his great-grandmother in front of a pyramid, so Platt thinks the coral Egyptian cat came from Egypt.

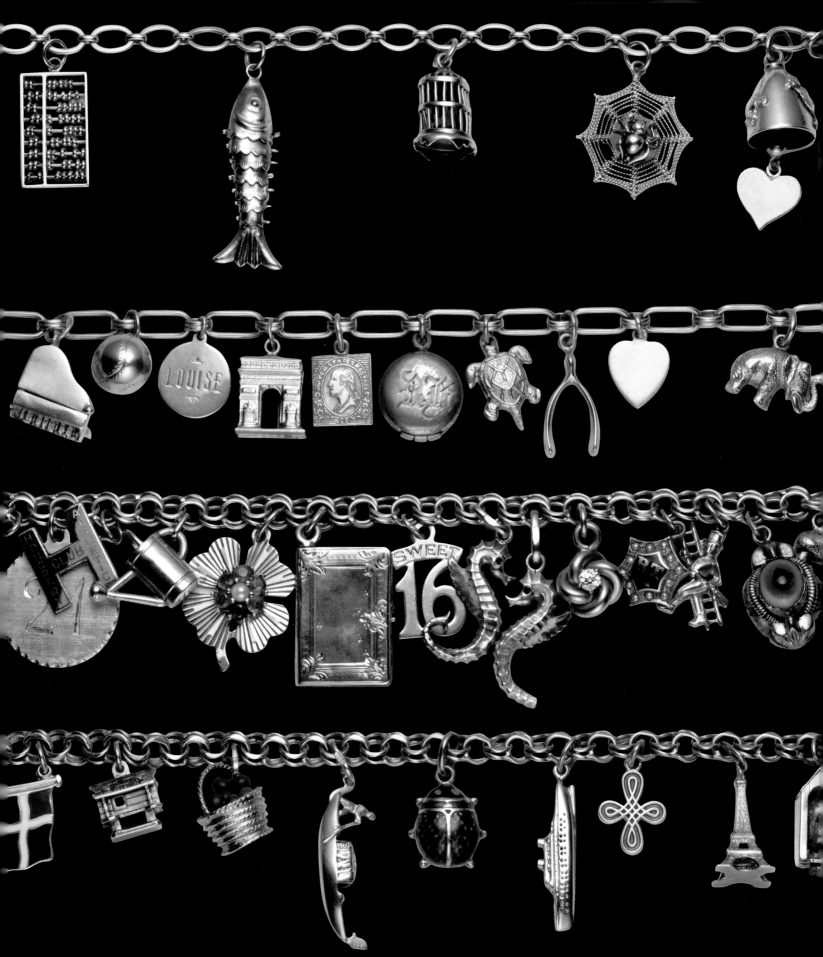

◀ A number of years ago, pottery designer Louise Jenks hooked all four of her charm bracelets together and started wearing them as a necklace. "It is a great conversation piece," says Jenks, "but sometimes I have to make up a story or two about the origins of the charms, because who has a memory quite that sharp?" Jenks is partial to the Asian-themed bracelet (top) because her father picked out all the charms himself and gave it to her just before he died. Next is her "mishmash" bracelet that includes a turtle (her nickname), a baseball ("because we are Cincinnati Reds fans"), and a 100-year-old family locket. The third bracelet includes Jenks' sorority pins, both Sweet 16 and twenty-first birthday charms, and her grandmother's book locket. Jenks assembled the last bracelet herself with souvenirs from trips to Europe.

▶ "It was right after September 11, 2001, and everyone was looking into their family histories, so I decided to make each of my daughters a charm bracelet," recalls Leslie Slutksy (right). "People commented about their bracelets everywhere they went." Thus began her one-of-a-kind charm bracelet business, called C.H.A.R.M., which stands for "charms have a real meaning," which she is running with her daughter, Lisa (left). With an inventory of more than 4,000 trinkets, Leslie and Lisa put together bracelets based on information gleaned from a detailed survey that each customer completes. C.H.A.R.M.'s company motto is "Life is too short NOT to wear it on your sleeve."

▲ Like most charm bracelet lovers, home furnishings magnate Chris Madden received her first bracelet—with a single, monogrammed heart charm—from her mother. The bracelet's initials stand for Madden's given name, Ann Christine Casson, and the other charms from her youth include ballet slippers to commemorate a performance of *The Nutcracker,* a memento from a prom, and a megaphone as a reminder of high school. Madden also collects cameos, and when she saw a black-and-white cameo charm at an antique show, she quickly added it to her bracelet.

▲ "I never meant for this to be a business," says Wells Jenkins, a former architect and the founder of Wells-Ware, a celebrated, one-of-a-kind charm company. Her charms encase photos and other personal keepsakes in tiny silver frames that, when strung together on a necklace or bracelet, tell her clients' stories like a portable photographic flipbook. Here Wells is pictured with her dog, Miss Pearl, who wears a charm with Wells' picture around her neck while Wells has a picture of Miss Pearl on her bracelet.

▶ A bevy of photographic charms by Wells Jenkins, who has built a business, Wells-Ware, around this personal style of charm. Among those who have commissioned her unique pieces are Paul Newman, Oprah Winfrey, Sting, Katie Couric, and Toni Morrison. "Wells creates charms that make life's milestones more special," says Chris Madden, whose own personal charms appear at right. "I think life is about creating sanctuaries . . . whether it's a house, a private room, or a charm bracelet."

◄ "Most jewelry is about memories," says noted astrologist Cheryl Lee Terry, who built a following with years' worth of columns for *Elle* magazine and, more recently, for *TimeOut* weekly. "I wore this all of the time," she says, pulling her silver charm bracelet out of her jewelry box and clasping the heart charm nearest the bracelet's clasp. "This shiny heart was my first charm, and for a while I wore it around my neck. It was from my very best friend," she recalls. After reviewing all 30 charms, including a three-pence coin from 1945 that her parents brought home after World War II, a worry bird that got her through exams, a bauble from cheerleading, an award from the Girl Scouts, her father's football charm from 1943, plus lots of charms from boyfriends, Terry concludes, "My youth is on this bracelet."

► A yard of charms! When he learned that we were creating this book, a London-based friend of New York jewelry collector Ralph Esmerian offered this amazing collection of charms dating back to the mid-19th century. When the circle is unwound, it reveals a collection of bracelets and belts that stretch for more than three feet. One of the owner's favorite charms is the little yellow egg (seen at about the nine o'clock position in the photo). The small stone encased in wire (just below the egg) is a piece of a bomb from the London blitz during World War II.

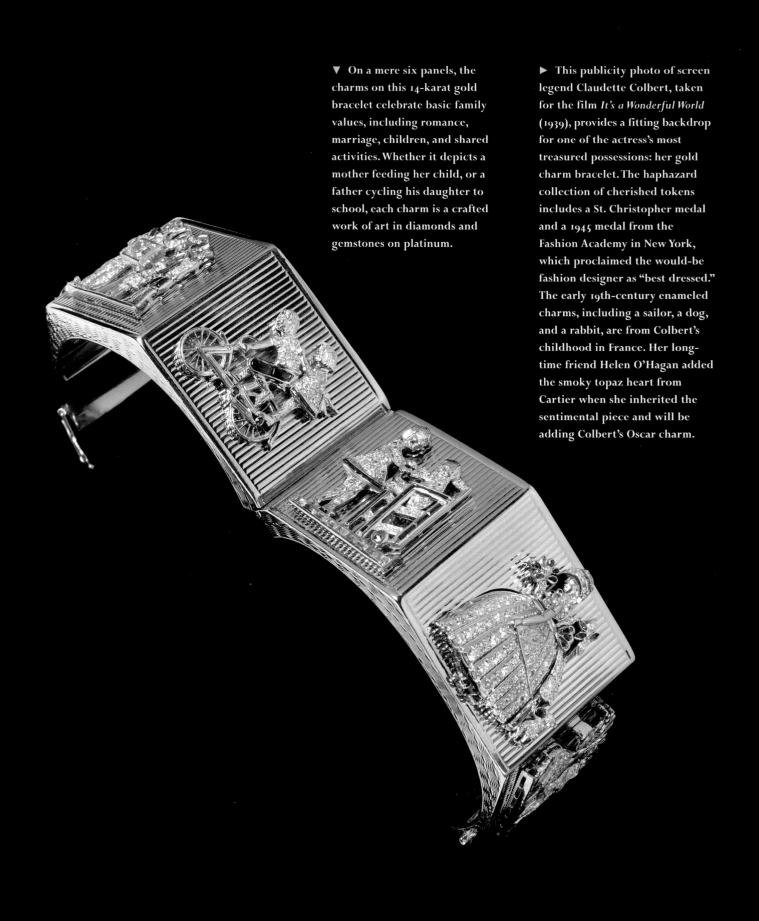

▼ On a mere six panels, the charms on this 14-karat gold bracelet celebrate basic family values, including romance, marriage, children, and shared activities. Whether it depicts a mother feeding her child, or a father cycling his daughter to school, each charm is a crafted work of art in diamonds and gemstones on platinum.

► This publicity photo of screen legend Claudette Colbert, taken for the film *It's a Wonderful World* (1939), provides a fitting backdrop for one of the actress's most treasured possessions: her gold charm bracelet. The haphazard collection of cherished tokens includes a St. Christopher medal and a 1945 medal from the Fashion Academy in New York, which proclaimed the would-be fashion designer as "best dressed." The early 19th-century enameled charms, including a sailor, a dog, and a rabbit, are from Colbert's childhood in France. Her long-time friend Helen O'Hagan added the smoky topaz heart from Cartier when she inherited the sentimental piece and will be adding Colbert's Oscar charm.

incredible journeys Few souvenirs can so effectively summon forth memories of a romantic tryst in a far-flung locale, or a once-in-a-lifetime adventure, than a beautiful charm. "You go shopping when you travel in order to bring back the spirit of the place you visited. It makes your trip more meaningful," says New York–based travel writer Mary Alice Kellogg. "I bring back things by local artisans, and jewelry always helps recall your experiences. Charms are tangible expressions of an intangible path. And the fun of finding them is also part of those memories." Some people turn the search for charms into a full-time hobby. They travel often and enjoy assembling international charm bracelets. Others use charms as thank-you gifts to express their love and appreciation for shared vacations in different parts of the world. Most of us just *like* charms and look for them wherever we happen to be. Some "travel" charms are not souvenirs as much as they are amulets carried to protect travelers on their journeys. A surprising number of people report having a lucky or protective token tucked away whenever they are on the road. Jewelry designer Elizabeth Locke, for example, will not even enter a car without her "lucky pearl." In the 1950s, St. Christopher medals were ubiquitous guardians of safe travel. Other charm aficionadas, such as New York socialite Nan Kempner find comfort on every flight—especially during takeoffs and landings—in clutching lucky charms that include a gold figure her daughter made, a lucky red chili pepper from Italian designer Valentino, a pre-Columbian charm, and a coin blessed by the pope.

▶ Paris is a popular travel destination, but as the owner of this bracelet says: "I had never seen a Paris-themed charm bracelet quite like this." Typically, you get an Eiffel Tower (this charm is so popular that Rembrandt Charms makes it in three sizes), plus maybe the Arc de Triomphe. But in addition to these two classics, this bracelet includes (from left): the Madeleine, the back of the Paris Opera, St. Chapelle, and the neighborhood church of St.-Germain-des-Prés.

◄ New York artist Marilla Palmer Zaremba wears 19 of her growing collection of charm bracelets. She assembled her first one when she was 10 years old, during a grand tour of Europe with her aunt. "My second wave of charm-bracelet building began in the early 1980s, when I met my husband," she explains, referring to rock star Peter Zaremba, lead singer and keyboardist for The Fleshtones. "His band travels a lot, and he brings individual charms back to me. He put together a good one from Australia that includes a platypus, a boomerang, and Ned Kelly—the famous Aussie outlaw. When we travel together, we hunt for charms. We've assembled some other really nice bracelets from our adventures. The Guatemalan one is one of the best, with Mayan figurines, and the tiny crown from a small saint icon that we had made into a charm."

▼ This bracelet takes you on a whirlwind tour of architectural wonders around the world— from the Acropolis in Athens and an Egyptian pyramid to the Empire State Building. It also features Westminster Abbey, the Lincoln Memorial, the Alamo, the League of Nations building in Geneva, and the Leaning Tower of Pisa. (The Washington Monument and Sacré Coeur are out of sight.) The Swiss chalet that opens to reveal a fondue pot is a favorite charm of owner Marilla Palmer Zaremba.

◄ The late Puff Rice, banker Joe Mansfield's longtime lady love, was a well-known travel agent whose celebrity clients included Jackie Onassis. Rice and Mansfield's romance was marked by adventures. Everywhere the pair went, Mansfield would purchase a charm on the sly, or have a jeweler he knew customize one, and present it to her upon their return. The result is this necklace. London Bridge marks their first trip. Other charms spark memories of European vacations, including a stay in the King's Suite of their hotel in Prague. An anchor charm commemorates a Mediterranean cruise, a smart airplane recalls five Concorde voyages, and a pin summons memories of an African safari.

► This beautiful bracelet was owned by the mother of architecture and interior design author Suzanne Slesin. "My mother was very superstitious," she explains. "I don't know how her association with this bracelet got started, but my mother would never go on a trip without it." The mainstay of the bracelet is the set of jeweled watch fobs, which were very popular in the 1950s. Slesin gave her mother the key charm. The rest of the charms represent wishes for a happy voyage and a safe return.

◄ The ivory, tortoiseshell, and rose gold charms on this enchanting music-and-animal-themed bracelet have a restrained palette and stylized quality. In part because of the materials used in the charms, a gentle sound emanates from the bracelet when it is worn.

► Home furnishings executive Sherri Donghia, who especially likes handmade ethnic jewelry, spotted this charm necklace made of natural ivory, bone, and horn in a shop in East Hampton, New York. She was particularly drawn to the carved ivory egg with a baby chick peeking out. Although she is not certain, Donghia believes that "someone who traveled through the Middle East, the Far East, and India must have put it together herself. I like to think that she was one of the rare breed of trailblazing Western women who traveled the Silk Road with her possessions rolled into small fabric bundles. There have been some brave women in our past."

▼ The colorful crests on this vintage enamel bracelet spell out "Hello Hawaii." Or is it "Good-bye"? Either way, it's "Aloha."

► Charms from the New York City Transit Museum gift shop reflect the exuberance and style that is quintessentially New York City. Counterclockwise from left: the Chrysler Building; a New York City transit token, a mass transit mainstay from 1958 until it was eliminated in 2003; the Empire State Building; a sign saying "New York" with an apple replacing the letter "O" as a play on New York's famous moniker, the Big Apple; the Flatiron Building; and the Brooklyn Bridge.

▲ Forget buying postcards! Hit the open road with the top down and, along the way, collect charms like these from each state.

of politics and patriots Patriotic and political motifs remain a potent unifying force, especially during times of crisis. Trinkets bearing nationalistic symbols, such as Old Glory, bald eagles, and presidential campaign buttons, have a special place in the history of American decorative arts, including our charm heritage. World War II engendered new kinds of charms—some for soldiers, and others for sweethearts and families looking for ways to show their love and support for those on the battlefront. Tiny plastic charms were tucked into letters, expressing cheerful sentiments and serving as little talismans for men in the trenches. In finer fashion, Tiffany saluted those in the services by offering 14-karat gold charms in the shape of airplanes, tanks, military insignia, and other images symbolizing the war. Charms migrated stateside when soldiers and sailors returned home with souvenir charms for their loved ones, including gold and silver replicas of the Eiffel Tower, to complete charm bracelets embodying their tour of duty. Military insignia and emblems not made specifically as charms were often put to use as charm jewelry. Buttons from military uniforms were affixed to chain bracelets, and tokens recalling a son's valor in war were worn on chains by proud mothers. Prominent figures in American political life also wore charms to symbolize their civic service. Clare Booth Luce created necklaces that illustrated her career as a correspondent and diplomat. Many First Ladies have enjoyed charms: Mamie Eisenhower was often photographed wearing them; style-conscious Jacqueline Kennedy Onassis owned several charm bracelets; Senator Hillary Clinton has a bracelet displaying New York State landmarks; and California's First Lady, Maria Shriver, has developed a collection of photographic charms depicting California landmarks and is giving a portion of the proceeds from the sales of the charms to charity.

▲ Small clusters of cherries, portraits of George Washington, American flags, medallions, and flag-waving cherubs (all created on *découpage* paper-over-cardboard), coupled with red, white, and blue beads, result in a bracelet that's a lighthearted salute to the Fourth of July.

▲ Medals of honor are the charms of distinguished service, whether for military bravery or for contributions to the arts and education. Shown here are three French awards, collected onto one gold chain. The prestigious *Légion d'honneur*, or French Legion of Honor Award (left), was instituted by Napoleon Bonaparte in 1804 to reward virtue, honor, and heroism in the service of France. The award is not reserved exclusively for military valor, but also has been conferred upon artists, scholars, and other esteemed personalities, including a few non-French people, including Julia Child and Charlie Chaplin. The *Croix de Guerre* (center) was created in 1915 to recognize acts of courage in the face of enemies during World War I, and was reinstituted at the start of World War II. The *Palmes Académiques* (right), also created by Napoleon Bonaparte in 1808, is the oldest honor available to ordinary citizens. Also known as the "Purple Legion," it recognizes teachers and others for academic merit, including contributions to the promotion of French language, culture, and educational activities.

▶ When Paris fell to the Germans in 1940, Louis Cartier commented by offering a brooch called "*L'occupation*." Trapped in a cage with bowed head, a downcast gemstone bird was a clear metaphor for the plight of Parisians. In celebration of the Nazi retreat in 1944, the jeweler introduced "*La Libération*." This time, the songbird announced his freedom from the open door of his cage. Here is Cartier's current version of the birdcage, a charm rendered in pavé diamonds, emerald, and 18-karat gold.

◄ During World War II, families, friends, and lovers at home could buy little charms like these to enclose in letters they sent to their loved ones on the front lines.

► During World War II, soldiers and their sweethearts could be separated for years, and giving loved ones a keepsake was a popular way to keep the home fires burning. Author and passionate collector Nick Snider has accumulated more than ten thousand "sweetheart" collectibles, and in July 2004, opened the National Museum of Patriotism in Atlanta, to preserve these pieces of Americana. Each branch of the military service produced a broad selection of charm jewelry using military seals and other tokens. The button-bedecked charm bracelet, known as a "Conquest Bracelet" (top) has a particularly fascinating story. According to tradition, each brass button represents a soldier with whom the owner had "served time" (Snider's euphemism for making love). Snider insists that the eighty-one-year-old woman in Birmingham, Alabama, who sold him this bracelet remembered every single one of her men!

◄ A World War II commemorative charm bracelet, set upon a keepsake-embroidered handkerchief.

◄ Michele Oka Doner is an artist known for her public art works. Her bracelet is from the 1940s, and was an anniversary gift to her mother from her father. One charm is the key to the city of Miami Beach (her father was the mayor from 1957 to 1964); another piece symbolizes the Miss Universe contest, which her mother hosted for years. "My mother's bracelet is about traveling and being a greeter to the world. (Miami Beach was then, as it is now, an international playground.) For my father, the bracelet was about sentiment. But my mother wasn't sentimental. For her, the bracelet was about power. The charms were her trophies."

◀ In this informal photograph with her future husband, taken shortly after they were engaged, Jackie Kennedy is wearing a classic charm bracelet with three hearts and a medallion. The simplicity of the bracelet is entirely in keeping with Jackie's stylish yet traditional elegance.

▶ In this vintage bracelet, golden peanuts that the Planters Peanuts Company sold at their stands in the 1950s are combined with a medallion from one of Jimmy Carter's campaigns for the presidency. Carter was himself a peanut farmer, so this bracelet works as an amusing political statement.

in style Some charm bracelets are more about style than sentiment. Take, for example, the ode to Coco Chanel's good luck symbols on bracelets and belts that Karl Lagerfeld introduced in the mid-1980s, or the diminutive shoe bracelet fashioned after classics from the Costume Institute at the Metropolitan Museum of Art in New York City. Fashion designer Marc Jacobs clearly spelled out a new style of charms when he introduced the first jewelry design—*Le Charm Bracelet*—for the French luxury fashion firm Louis Vuitton in 2001. With eleven French-themed charms, Jacobs triggered a revival of this sentimental type of jewelry and brought sexiness, sophistication, and corporate flag waving (why not?) to a whole new era of charmed jewelry. With a price tag of almost $6,000, the high-fashion charm bracelet was reborn. Soon, charm bracelets were seen on the runways from Dolce & Gabbana in Milan to Anna Sui in New York, and on such celeb fashionistas as Demi Moore, Chlöe Sevigny, and Sarah Jessica Parker. Firms as varied as Marni and Burberry added charm bracelets to their inventory, while venerable jewelry houses like Cartier and Garrard reissued some of their classics and introduced brand-new charm motifs. Tiffany recently backed a dazzling new line of romantic, historically inspired jewelry from Temple St. Clair Carr, the latest design darling for the venerable firm. Carr's pieces are grounded in the contemporary, but are inspired by the past, especially her signature egg-shaped medieval-style crystal amulets which evoke, of all people, Catherine de Médicis. Most new-style charms and charm bracelets—many of which are preassembled collections of motifs, rather than individual collectibles are decidedly modern, a far cry from their old-fashioned, super-sentimental forebears. Esteemed psychologist Dr. Joyce Brothers likes the idea of these modern alternatives. Although she has her own traditional charm bracelet, she believes "modern-day charms are about fashion. They often have built-in obsolescence. In the past, we passed down charms because they were not only beautiful, but because we hoped that sentimentality would resonate from generation to generation. However, these types of charms require storage and care. Today, we want to wear something new and fabulous."

◄ Coco Chanel understood the power and importance of accessories, including charms that continue to enliven the Chanel jewelry collection to this day. Oversized charms on necklaces, bracelets, and belts from the 1980s were designed with cheeky irreverence by Karl Lagerfeld, the creative force behind Chanel since 1983. Here, a belt features Mademoiselle's iconic "5," a miniature replica of the Chanel No. 5 perfume bottle, a medallion bearing her favored five-pointed star, and a miniature of her signature quilted handbag. Legend has it that in 1921, when the perfume chemist Ernest Beaux created sample fragrances, Coco selected the fifth blend he submitted, and called it simply Chanel No. 5. Thereafter, five became her lucky number.

◄ When Cornelia Guest was nine years old, her mother, the late socialite and gardening expert C. Z. Guest, gave her a delicate gold bracelet with nine little charms in various colors. (The white charm is centered with a sapphire.) The bracelet was simplicity itself; just the kind of jewelry a young girl could cherish—and just the sort her mother preferred. But C.Z. also admired quality, and these charms are tiny Fabergé enameled eggs that C. Z.'s husband, Winston, had given her over the years. "My father just loved Fabergé eggs," says Cornelia. Happily, the bracelet still fits, and Cornelia still wears her eggs, especially when she feels sentimental.

► Although jewelry designer James Taffin de Givenchy (his uncle is Hubert de Givenchy) is busy with his own designs for his Taffin Collection, he sometimes helps a customer with a piece that she already owns and cherishes. One such client, inspired by the jewelry of the late Line Vautrin, spent several years working with designer Richard Robinson to create this beautiful bracelet. Givenchy added a Burmese peridot wrapped in an 18-karat gold ribbon, and is working on other charm designs.

◄ Established in 1735, Garrard, the venerable London-based jeweler, is most famous for bejeweling the royal family. Following a recent trend of infusing established brands with youthful energy and vision, the firm, in 2002, installed Jade Jagger (daughter of Mick and Bianca) as the firm's creative director. Under her aegis, Garrard introduced charms and pendants for chain-link bracelets and necklaces, including this series of reinvented royal symbols, such as swords, crests, shields, crowns, and medallions. Employing 14-karat gold, enamel, and diamonds, they are produced to Garrard's high standard of craftsmanship and luxury.

► When Louis Vuitton launched its first jewelry collection in 2001, Marc Jacobs was at the helm bringing youth, charisma, and downtown élan to the venerable label. Many credit *Le Charm Bracelet*—the most talked-about piece from the debut collection—with having started the charm bracelet craze that has followed. Jacobs' bracelet collects a series of iconic status symbols: tiny versions of the coveted LV handbags, such as the classic Alma style done in onyx and 18-karat gold. Other charms pertain to the world of wealth, privilege, and indulgence that is inhabited by glamorous jet-setters who tote Louis Vuitton luggage.

▲ For the 1999 holiday season, cosmetics company Estée Lauder introduced a special collection of mirrored powder compacts accessorized with a series of coordinating charms. It was an irresistible combination. Eight charms, all made of gold-plated brass with lead crystal details, include baby shoes, a gift box, a star, a heart, and a diamond ring. Evelyn Lauder, president of the company, says that she loves to keep charms to remind her of events throughout her life or to symbolize passions.

▶ Who knew that you could toy with something as traditional as a charm bracelet? These fabulous if-you've-got-it-flaunt-it earrings are a clever spin-off of one of Louis Vuitton's own charm bracelet designs. The ancients wore earrings as amulets to deliver them from evil and carry good luck. Today, we wear earrings for reasons much less mystical, but these jingling baubles hint at another kind of magic: the magic of charming luxury.

▲ Jewelry designer David Yurman once made an angel charm as a donation to Elton John's AIDS foundation. "It wasn't intended as a gold charm that we would sell, but people kept requesting it," says Yurman, stating proudly that the first round of sales produced more than $50,000 for John's foundation. To celebrate the 25th anniversary of his family business in 2004, Yurman assembled some of the components from his designs over the years and decided to make a charm bracelet. "That's what charm bracelets are all about," he says. "They connect you to the past." On the anniversary bracelet are a diamond-encircled amethyst, a blue topaz, a pearl drop, diamond hearts, and an angel charm hanging from airy gold links.

◄ For the truly fashionable, no ordinary wristwatch will do. No, it is much more creative—and eye-catching—to adorn yourself with a pendant watch, worn on a twisted gold link chain. Verdura's delectable pineapple timepiece is photographed alongside an original sketch for the design from the 1950s. Part of a sketch for its mate—a dome-shaped hive with a jeweled bumblebee—appears at right. The circular watch pendant (above) bears Verdura's own signature. The square, diamond-studded watch, which Paul Flato designed for Verdura, is a whimsical play on a padlock.

◄ Jewelry designer Pedro Boregaard holds his personal amulet—a smooth piece of a tree branch that snapped off in his hand one evening when he and a friend discovered that, after a long walk in the country, they had ended up on the edge of a steep cliff after nightfall with no apparent way down. "I studied the ground and took my best guess. We found out later that if we had taken any other route, we would have fallen straight down." When Boregaard finally reached safety, he noticed that he was still clutching the little piece of wood. "I keep it to remind me that there's always a way. A situation is only hopeless when you think it is."

► "When I first did my eggs, I was thinking of creating a collection of textures, not the motif itself," says Munich-born artisan/jeweler Pedro Boregaard, who spent seven years designing jewelry for Tiffany. "Every jeweler in Europe has little egg charms. They are symbols of regeneration, and they have a shape that anyone can understand and relate to. That is one of the key elements of a good charm. When I started my business in 1988, I spent three months making a big neck-lace with forty-eight different eggs. I liked the idea that all these little charms together formed an important piece of jewelry."

just for fun   Sometimes we take our wardrobes, our jewelry, and even ourselves a little too seriously. We need to lighten up! So, why not put Snow White, Mickey Mouse, or Hello Kitty on the job?   Toward that end, in 2004, designer Miuccia Prada came up with toy-like charms known as "tricks." This series of witty charms depicted Prada's classic stilettos and signature bowling ball handbag, as well as butterflies and hearts. In addition, Miuccia created Annabelle, Hook, and Pinky, a multidimensional robot collection, to bring out the child in all of us. These charms are displayed on T-shirts, briefcases, key chains, and even Christmas trees. In similar fashion, designer Caterina Zangrando creates layered necklaces with strands of pearls, little metal charms, and cartoon motifs, while newcomer Gabriel Urist expresses his hoop dreams with basketball-inspired polished metal charms featuring slam dunkers in silhouette.   Charms add humor to last year's dignified handbag, sass to a lackluster belt or bracelet, and warmth to cold personal electronics like our ubiquitous cell phones. Whether they are gold-enameled cartoon characters from Cartier, a jolly parade of Christmas ornaments on a necklace, or vintage trinkets from a Cracker Jack box, charms meant "just for fun" inject a dose of joy into our hyper-serious lives.

◀ Under extreme stress, the body of Marvel comic book character Bruce Banner morphs into the Hulk. This super-masculine form is the ideal model for a trio of charms from jewelry designer Ara. The Strong Arm fist charm (left) is the embodiment of his company's maxim—"Stay strong. Be cool." The crescent moon pendant (right) symbolizes the natural world. The key (center) reflects a more personal inspiration: As a child, Ara had a cupboard that could be opened only by using a special key. These three charms are as personally expressive as they are simple, and their powerful presence is enough to make even the Hulk turn green with envy.

◄ When twins get together, it's double the fun! The Johnston twins, Alison and Brooke, are regular models for photographer Jade Albert. Embodiments of the adage that blondes have more fun, here they merrily show off their enameled charm bracelets from The Gap.

◄ Fashion historian Caroline Rennolds Milbank is a passionate collector of designer accessories, as is demonstrated in her book *The Couture Accessory*. Milbank admires both the old school (Chanel) and the new school (Marc Jacobs). This quirky suspension of doll-like figures, created by the hip Italian design house Marni, is one of the newer additions to Milbank's personal collection.

► Actress Hallie Eisenberg has many of the interests of a normal 12-year-old—her dogs, rollerblading, and charm bracelets. Dangling from her right wrist is the bracelet that her movie double, Hayley, gave her after filming *The Goodbye Girl* (2004). The charms include French fries (a little joke between the two girls), a suitcase, Rollerblades, and a silver and rhinestone "H" for their shared initial. On her left wrist is one of the modular bracelets that are popular today among the tween set. "My agent gave it to me for my birthday," says Eisenberg. "My friends have them, too, and sometimes we trade for the day."

◄ The St. John company, known for its elegant knitwear, launched its first jewelry collection in 1987. Today, Marie Gray, the company's founder and head designer, still develops each new piece and oversees its execution. Here, a charm necklace strung with an array of brightly colored Christmas tree ornaments makes a sparkling accessory for holiday parties.

► Juicy Couture designers Pamela Skaist-Levy and Gela Taylor have a clear vision of the woman who wears their edgy-but-sophisticated clothes. The team recently offered their smart, sassy customers a line of Juicy accessories, and the main attraction of their jewelry collection was this charm bracelet. The strawberries, crowns, hearts, coins, good luck symbols, and other trinkets—even a Juicy surfboard—are as lighthearted as they are colorful.

▼ Talk about branding! In the 1940s and 1950s, companies gave away commercial souvenirs like these in hopes of charming customers into coming back to their products again and again. Here are a few of those trinkets, including a Pet Evaporated Milk can, a Canada Dry Ginger Ale bottle, a Heinz vinegar jar, a Diamond Crystal salt box, and a 7-Up bottle, all in plastic on a gold chain bracelet.

▶ In the early 1990s, Rembrandt Charms, the Buffalo-based specialty charm manufacturer that produces 9,000 different charm motifs, began promoting themed charms bracelets. Some of the perennial favorites are Christmas motifs, music icons, gardening tools, and nautical symbols. The kitchen helper here serves up 14-karat gold replicas of kitchen tools, from a stand-up mixer to a measuring cup, a colander—even a cleaver.

SURPRISE INSIDE

GUESS WHAT'S INSIDE

Fold And Tear Here

◄ Cracker Jack candied popcorn introduced its concept of "a prize in every box" in 1912. In the 1920s, the company began using little "pot metal" or plastic charms for prizes in some of the boxes, and a new charm craze was born. Here are examples from the 1920s to the 1960s, including a sledgehammer, binoculars, a typewriter, a poodle, and a camera.

The pebbled plastic "dangles" were created as a series of twelve charms by C. Carey Cloud, the most prolific of the Cracker Jack charm designers. According to diehard collector Jim Davis, chief of the official Cracker Jack Web site and owner of these charms, the sugary confection is just "edible packing material" for the charms.

▼ Hip New York jewelry designer Gabriel Urist has been playing basketball all his life. Here, he is holding one of his own well-worn basketballs draped with his charmed jewelry, all basketball motifs. These silhouettes capture in gold and silver (and occasionally with pearls for the basketballs) the quintessential moments of athletic power and grace on the court.

◀ Fashion designer Betsey Johnson is a charm aficionada. She wears charms on a chain around her neck and sometimes braids them into her hair. Every item in Johnson's recent lingerie collection is trimmed with a charm.

▶ Johnson's beloved celluloid charms from the 1930s and 1940s, which she found in a thrift shop, have been incorporated into the décor of her weekend home in East Hampton, New York. They live on a pink ribbon and have enjoyed several places of honor in Johnson's home.

▲ *Snow White and The Seven Dwarfs* (1938) was the first animated feature film ever made and, not surprisingly, inspired all sorts of merchandise. What actually may be surprising is that Cartier formed a licensing agreement with Walt Disney Productions that ran from 1937 to 1942, and produced magnificent enameled gold charms featuring Disney characters. This *Snow White* charm bracelet, circa 1938, is a beguiling example of the collaboration. All the bracelets bearing the Disney charms were cherished by children and grown-ups alike, and remain "hot items" among jewelry collectors.

◄ This brilliant platinum kiss, covered with almost three carats of diamonds, is what designers Carl and Elizabeth Ferrara call "the sweetest kiss in the world." As Elizabeth says, "It has lots of carats . . . but no calories." It is just one of the many different kinds of no-cal Hershey kisses made by their firm, J&C Ferrara.

► In 1978, entertainer and society matron Kitty Carlisle Hart, a Radcliffe parent, hosted a gala dinner during the centennial celebration for the college, and President Matina S. Horner gave her a shiny gold police whistle as a thank-you gift. "My whistle is my lucky charm. I wear it all the time," exclaims the 94-year-old former chairwoman of the New York State Council of the Arts, who still sings classic American show tunes at cabaret gigs. Hart says that her goal now is to live to be 103, ". . . to see my grandchildren through school."

bling! "Bling," a slang word introduced around the year 2000, describes the outsized, ostentatious jewelry popularized by rappers and hip-hop artists. Taking its name from the title of the song *Bling Bling* by the rap group Cash Money Millionaires, the term is a hip, urban expression that encompasses everything from David Beckham's earrings to the big, bold, diamond-encrusted baubles that Jacob the Jeweler, the father of bling, has made for celebs like the late Notorious B.I.G. and Lil' Kim. Not surprisingly, bling has become part of our everyday lexicon—it is fun to say, fun to fantasize about, and fun to feel a part of the hard-edged glamour it suggests. Even Donald Trump spoofed the concept when for a recent cover of *Esquire* he layered huge glittering medallions around his neck spelling out "Trump," and "Moneyman" and "Big D." Bling's dramatic scale, materials, and prices are perfectly suited to today's vastly influential music industry and its larger-than-life music stars. But, in truth, bling has been around the music biz for decades. Liberace, an icon of the 1950s, was recently dubbed "The King of Bling" by *W Magazine,* and of course Elvis, while firmly entrenched as the King of Rock and Roll, might easily be considered the Duke of Bling. Even the awesome Pearl Bailey showed off a bit of bling on occasion, as do a number of somewhat "quieter" bling aficionadas.

▶ These jazz musician charms from the 1930s are museum-quality precursors to today's bling jewelry. "It is the most beautiful charm bracelet that I have ever seen," declares jewelry expert Ralph Esmerian about this Art Deco platinum, sapphire, diamond, ruby, citrine, and emerald jazz orchestra charm bracelet. "The stones are well crystallized and beautifully cut. The design of the players is simple, very modern, and very bold. It is beautifully conceived and executed, and it certainly signifies the period."

▼ On Elvis Presley's 42nd birthday, the King of Rock and Roll received this blue enamel-and-diamond pendant with gold symbols representing each of the 12 zodiac signs. The piece was created by New York designer Peter Lindeman. As Lindeman tells it: "One day, I got a call from someone at the Las Vegas Hilton Hotel, asking if I could put a plate on the back of my zodiac pendant so that it could be engraved for a very famous person, and if I could set the diamond arrow to indicate a Capricorn born on January 8. My birthday is also January 8, so I wanted to know who it was for." Needless to say, Lindeman was thrilled that he shared his birthday with the King, and that he was asked to design this special charm.

▶ Known throughout the world as "Mr. Showmanship," Liberace, who once wore a two-hundred-pound "King Neptune" costume covered in shells and pearls to a recital, had an equally remarkable jewelry box. The rest of us have had to make do with a bit less bling, like this Liberace-themed bracelet, complete with charms of his piano and his signature candelabra. Available in stores in the early 1950s, a time when the flamboyant pianist's television program was at its peak, this was just costume jewelry made of gold-plated metal, and cost about five dollars.

◄ Singing and acting legend Pearl Bailey is shown here before a concert at London's famed Talk of the Town cabaret in September, 1966, wearing a trio of classic 1950s-style fine gold charm bracelets. This extraordinarily stylish entertainer, who performed before seven United States presidents, claimed to dislike "anything phony"— including costume jewelry.

▶ The Cool Cat Orchestra features eight (three shown here) 14-karat gold feline musicians and a kittenish chanteuse. Erwin Dankner, co-owner of Henry Dankner & Sons, a jewelry firm specializing in charms, conceived the idea during a ride through the Tunnel of Music at the New York World's Fair in 1964. Some of the playful details on Dankner's creations include the bass fiddle player's tail that sticks out of the tails of his jacket and the tilted stand-up microphone for the chanteuse.

▲ "My charm bracelet was presented originally to my step-grandmother at the end of a *This Is Your Life* television show honoring my grandfather on March 19, 1961," says Lynn Jeffrey. Jeffrey watched her grandfather's appearance right from the audience. Her grandfather, Harry Ruby, was half of the songwriting team known from 1920 to 1947 as Kalmar and Ruby. His bracelet commemorates the team's hits, such as "A Kiss to Build a Dream On" and the classic "I Wanna Be Loved by You." The bracelet also honors Ruby's lifelong love of baseball, his children and grandchildren, his wife, and his early days peddling sheet music. The penny recalls Ruby's habit of picking up coins and keeping them in his "Found Money Box."

▶ Lynn Jeffrey wears one of the original *This Is Your Life* charm bracelets designed by Marchal Jewelers. Jeffrey's grandfather, songwriter Harry Ruby, was once featured on the program. Jeffrey is snuggling with her husband, Noel, one of New York's top-tier interior designers. Peeking out of his pocket is a blue enamel-and-gold Presbyterian Hospital Volunteer medal that he earned as a youngster. When he graduated from high school, he put his honor society buttons and other high school awards onto a bracelet as a gift for his mother, a sentimental keepsake that she passed down to Lynn.

◀ An antique Cartier watch and two shiny lamb charms—a curious pairing, but not for nine-year-old Storey, daughter of Helen Schifter, whose husband, Tim, is CEO of LeSportsac. The watch is a Schifter family heirloom, but the lambs are more recent finds. The lambs are from her new friend, rocker Gwen Stefani, who created the L.A.M.B. line of bags for LeSportsac (L.A.M.B. is an acronym for Stefani's favorite words: love, angel, music, and baby); each bag has a lamb charm. Mom Helen explains, "We like these three charms together because they represent the three members of our little family."

▶ Photographer Jade Albert found this quintessentially "bling" rhinestone alphabet at a novelty emporium associated with a popular New York gourmet sandwich shop called E.A.T.

◄ An assembly of diamond pendants, the ultimate bling, by designer to the rap stars, Jacob the Jeweler (a moniker affectionately given him by Sean "P. Diddy" Combs) Arabo. Jacob keeps legions of rap and rock royalty—along with other A-listers— dripping in diamonds that are worked onto pendants, crosses, and dog tags. He made the "J. Lo" pendant for Jennifer Lopez, a "JS" version for Jessica Simpson, and all sorts of baubles for R&B singer Faith Evans and her late husband, Notorious B.I.G.

▲ A cluster of dog tags by Richard Stark, owner of and designer for Chrome Hearts, jeweler to some of the music industry's hottest stars. The defiant mix of hard-edged motifs and luxe materials mirrors the company's image and clientele. Ozzy Osbourne, Steven Tyler, Lenny Kravitz, and Karl Lagerfeld are said to favor the firm's medieval-inspired jewelry and other accessories. Mick Jagger, who sometimes threads a bracelet through his lapel, was the

inspiration for the company's lips-and-tongue motif charm and other items that the company produced for the Rolling Stones. These dog tags borrow from traditional amuletic imagery: the cross promises protection; the dagger represents strength in medieval heraldry; the five-point star is associated with magic, protection, and good fortune; the fleur-de-lis, a French symbol of royalty, is associated with wisdom, femininity, fertility, and prosperity.

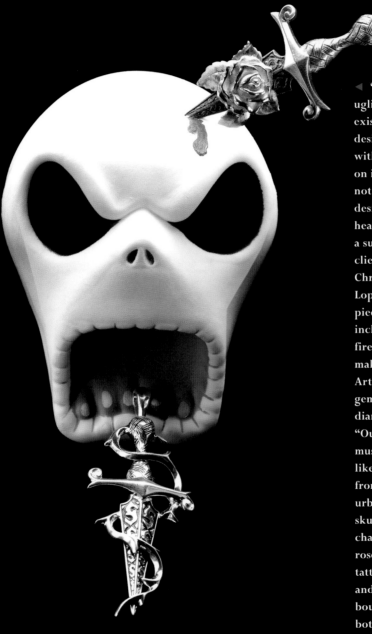

"We probably make the ugliest charm bracelet in existence," says British jewelry designer Stephen Webster, with a laugh, "because everything on it is a bit odd." What is not odd is how well Webster's designs have parlayed the heavy-metal goth aesthetic into a successful business. Famous clients, such as Ozzy Osbourne, Christina Aguilera, and Jennifer Lopez, have snatched up his lavish pieces. His repertoire which includes thorns, daggers, spikes, fire, wishbones, and stars, often makes oblique reference to Arthurian legends. Hefty cut gemstones and fields of pavé diamonds scream rock star glam. "Our image appeals to the music crowd," says Webster. "I like the idea of taking something from nature and giving it an urban edge." Here, piercing a toy skull, are two Stephen Webster charms: an 18-karat pink gold rose, inspired by the ornate tattoos associated with sailors and bikers, and an etched blade bound with a thorny vine, both of which seem lifted straight from the cover of a Guns N' Roses album.

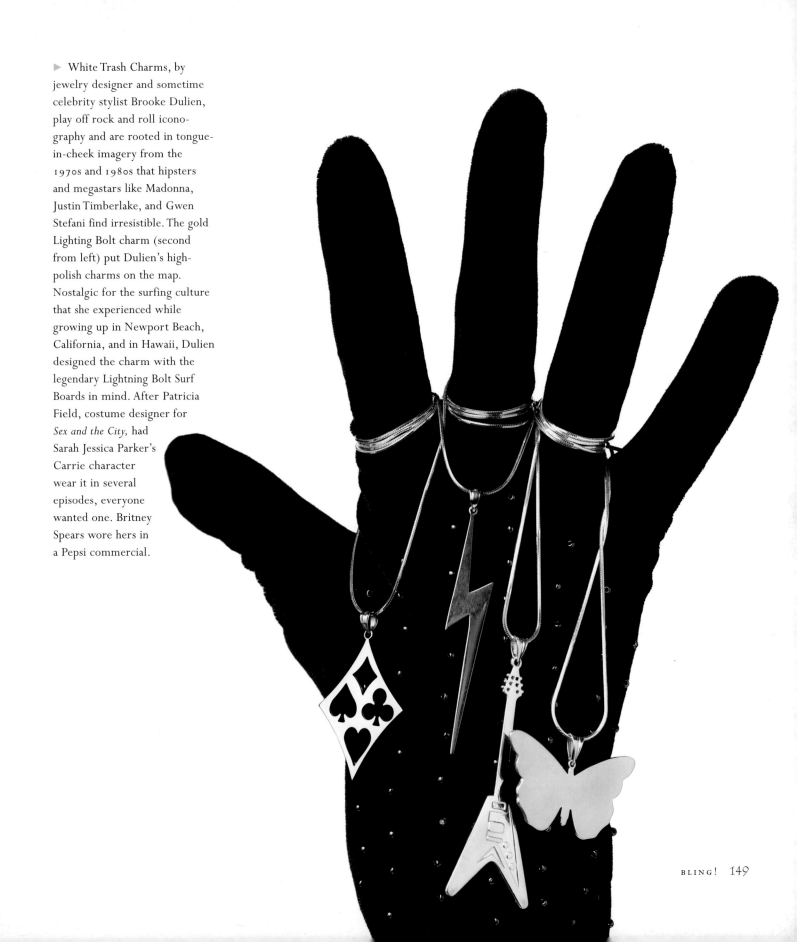

▶ White Trash Charms, by jewelry designer and sometime celebrity stylist Brooke Dulien, play off rock and roll iconography and are rooted in tongue-in-cheek imagery from the 1970s and 1980s that hipsters and megastars like Madonna, Justin Timberlake, and Gwen Stefani find irresistible. The gold Lighting Bolt charm (second from left) put Dulien's high-polish charms on the map. Nostalgic for the surfing culture that she experienced while growing up in Newport Beach, California, and in Hawaii, Dulien designed the charm with the legendary Lightning Bolt Surf Boards in mind. After Patricia Field, costume designer for *Sex and the City,* had Sarah Jessica Parker's Carrie character wear it in several episodes, everyone wanted one. Britney Spears wore hers in a Pepsi commercial.

the language of charms

Charms Communicate

A

AMETHYST
The birthstone for February is known to encourage sincerity, piety, and even celibacy. The ancients believed amethyst to be a strong antidote to drunkenness.

ANGEL
Angels are messengers of God, almighty spirits embodying goodness, mercy, justice, majesty, and wisdom.

ANKH
The ancient—and widely used—Egyptian precursor to the Christian cross, the ankh is a cross topped with a loop and is interpreted variously as a key, a tree of life, a knot, a phallus, and a sign of eternity.

AQUAMARINE
The birthstone for March, this sea-water blue stone is said to attract love and encourage new friendships. For married couples, the aquamarine is said to help promote a long, happy union.

B

BEAR
Classically aligned with Diana, goddess of the moon, the image of a bear (or its claws) is a symbol of diplomacy, strength, bravery, and physical and spiritual health and well-being. A bear or its claws are also said to assist a woman in childbirth.

BELL
Since ancient times, bells have been worn to combat the evil eye. In Exodus, Moses was instructed by God to affix bells to the hem of the vestments of high priests to thwart evil spirits.

BIRTHSTONES
Each month of birth is associated with one or more stones or materials. (See definitions for individual stones.)

January	Garnet
February	Amethyst
March	Aquamarine
April	Diamond
May	Emerald
June	Pearl (also Alexandrite)
July	Ruby
August	Peridot
September	Sapphire
October	Opal (or Tourmaline)
November	Topaz (or Citrine)
December	Turquoise (or Zircon)

BUDDHA
Buddha figurines symbolize happiness, kindness, and joy, and protect against sudden death. They also are said to bring wealth if their tummies are rubbed.

C

CAT
Cats embody mystery, playfulness, independence, sensuality, and self-confidence. They are a combination of the physical and the spiritual. The black cat is thought to possess magical powers, and, as a charm, is considered a lucky omen.

CORAL
Coral is thought to protect children, from harm, cure stomach and eye maladies, bring wisdom and reason, evoke flow and change in life, thwart the evil eye, and as Pliny once said, quiet tempests.

CROSS
Adopted as the symbol of Christianity as far back as the fourth century A.D., the cross was used for many centuries as a defense against evil spirits. In pagan societies dating back to at least 4,000 B.C., symbols similar to the simple Latin cross—that is, with a longer upright than crossbar—were considered to be phallic symbols.

CROWN
The symbol of royalty or the reward for victory in a sport or other contest.

D

DAISY

Daisies symbolize innocence. Like a human eye, this flower has a center that looks like a pupil, and at night, the flower closes its petals in rest.

DIAMOND

The birthstone for April, the diamond is the hardest of all gemstones. Diamonds symbolize invulnerability and incorruptibility, and are associated with love, marriage, joy, excellence, and purity.

DOG

Canines stand for fidelity, reliability, and watchfulness. In the Chinese zodiac, a person born in the Year of the Dog (2006, 20018, 2030, 2042, etc.) is honest, intelligent, loyal, reliable, and just.

DOLPHIN

Ancient Egyptian Copts decorated garments with dolphin motifs, which are thought to have symbolized salvation and protection. Ulysses considered the dolphin a symbol of love, devotion, and hard work. Today, the dolphin suggests skill in communication, intelligence, joy, and cooperation.

E

EGG

Eggs are ancient symbols of love and fertility. In a Christian context, the egg commemorates the resurrection of Christ. In the Greek Orthodox tradition, you crack red-dyed eggs against your neighbor's eggs in celebration of this joyous event.

ELEPHANT

In Hindu mythology, Ganesh, the elephant-headed son of Shiva and Parvati, is the remover of obstacles and the god of domestic harmony and prosperity. In general, elephants symbolize enormous strength, wisdom, courage, and success.

EMERALD

The birthstone for May, the emerald's green color symbolizes spring, fertility, and eternal youth, as well as honesty and tranquillity.

EVIL EYE

Evil forces leveled at an individual through a gaze. The concept of blocking the evil eye with an amuletic representation of an eye originated with the Sumerians and Egyptians. The traditional hue of evil eye amulets is blue; that eye color, uncommon in the Mediterranean and Middle East, must have seemed potentially evil.

F

FISH

Sumerians and Babylonians fashioned fish amulets that date back to approximately 2,500 B.C. Fish symbolize fertility, virility, wealth, and abundance.

FLOWERS

The "language of flowers," or the notion of giving individual flowers symbolic meaning, was developed to a great extent by the sentimental Victorians.

Traditional Flowers-of-the-Month

January	Carnation
February	Violet
March	Daffodil
April	Sweet Pea
May	Lily of the Valley
June	Rose
July	Larkspur
August	Gladiolus
September	Aster
October	Marigold
November	Chrysanthemum
December	Narcissus

FROG

To the ancient Egyptians, the frog represented fertility and regeneration, and frog amulets were often buried within the wrappings of a mummy to guarantee rebirth into the next life. Today, frog amulets are worn for positive energy and are associated with longevity.

G

GARNET
The birthstone for January symbolizes faith, loyalty, and truth, and is thought to help deflect evil thoughts and improve intelligence.

GOLDFISH
First bred in China, these members of the carp family are the bearers of good fortune, prosperity, beauty, and harmony. The Chinese words for goldfish mean gold and abundance.

H

HORN
Known as a *corno* or *cornicello*, the horn is a typically Roman charm that resembles a long, slim, curved chili pepper. When carved from red coral, gold, or silver, it is one Roman version of the evil eye, and is still in use today.

HORSESHOE
Horseshoes promise luck and protection—place them upward and your luck will never run out; downward and luck can pour over you.

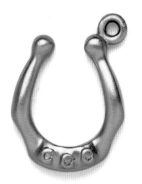

I

INSECTS
Common subjects for charms, many of which have symbolic meaning. (See Bee, Butterfly, Ladybug, Scarab.)

J

JADE
Used for amulets in Western Asia since 4,000 B.C., and also by ancient Egyptians and Aztecs, jade is thought to aid in childbirth and heal stomach and intestinal problems. It is associated with hope, faithfulness, and perfection. In China, jade is thought to promote prosperity.

K

KEY
A key can symbolize the opening of doors (to opportunity, for example, or knowledge) or the unlocking of secrets. A key is also a popular way to give your lover custody of your heart.

L

LADYBUG
The red ladybug is a time-honored harbinger of good luck.

LAMB
The lamb is a classic symbol of peace, and among Christians, it represents the body of Christ.

LAPIS LAZULI
Lapis lazuli, a blue-to-purplish stone, confers wisdom and creativity to those who wear it. It is also a symbol of royalty and fidelity. Its alchemic abilities include curing melancholy, sleeplessness, and dementia.

LION
The symbol of a lion promotes good health and prosperity, and it also is thought to be a valuable protector during travels. Lions also represent strength, bravery, and honor.

M

MOON
The moon, identified with the goddess Diana, offers the power to accomplish everyday chores. It is one of the governing planets of the zodiac. Crescent moons are thought to enhance moods, emotions, instincts, and intuition.

N

NUMBERS
Numbers have various meanings: "1" symbolizes God within the Holy Trinity and is the universal and transcendent number; "2" stands for existence and duality; "3" symbolizes the Holy Trinity as well as the three virtues—faith, hope, and charity; "4" is the number for balance and organization; "5" represents harmony and divine grace; "6" denotes longevity, and is also the number of evil; "7" represents luck, change, and positive renewal; "8" symbolizes perfection, prosperity, and infinity; "9" is the number for patience, mediation, and achievement; "10" incorporates all numbers and symbolizes harmony. (See Thirteen.)

ONYX

Onyx represents chastity and midnight. The stone is said to encourage good fortune, enhance self-control, and banish grief. In the Victorian era, onyx, because of its hue, was regarded as an appropriate stone for mourning jewelry.

OPAL

The birthstone for October, like the pearl, represents innocence and purity. For children, opals are believed to bring good fortune.

OWL

Owls represent wisdom, knowledge, truth, reason, and protection. Owl charms are given to honor an educational achievement.

P

PANSY

The pansy is associated with thoughts, memories, and merriment.

PEARL

The birthstone for June symbolizes innocence and purity. Pears also are associated with romance, love, and marriage, and are traditionally given on 12th or 20th wedding anniversaries. They are said to bring health and good luck.

PERIDOT

The birthstone for August is a symbol of good luck, success, and happiness and is believed to promote friendship and marriage. Because peridots seem to glow in the evening light, the ancients believed they protected their owners from danger at night.

PIG

Despite their less desirable present-day associations, pigs have long been a symbol of sincerity, honesty, reliability, intelligence, and kindness.

POMEGRANATE

The pomegranate is an ancient symbol of prosperity and fertility. Jackie Kennedy Onassis had a charm bracelet with a golden pomegranate in the center.

Q

QUINCE

A golden, apple-shaped fruit that may have been what Eve gave Adam in the Garden of Eden. The Greeks considered this fruit a symbol of desire and fertility.

R

RABBIT'S FOOT

The rabbit's mating habits made the animal a symbol of prosperity and fertility. Because they are born with their eyes open, they also are thought to ward off the evil eye.

ROSE

Ancient cultures valued this flower as a symbol of love, achievement, and perfection. Today, we associate this flower with love, passion, and respect (red rose), joy and friendship (yellow rose), gratitude and admiration (pink), and humility (white).

RUBY

The birthstone for July, the ruby (which means "red") is synonymous with power and passion. Rubies are thought to thwart evil, dispel sadness and discord, and protect their wearers from deceitful friendships.

S

SAPPHIRE

The birthstone for September symbolizes truth, sincerity, and the ability to make dreams come true. They also are thought to bring their wearers comfort, and constancy in marriage.

SCARAB

The scarab, a representation of the *scarabaeus sacer* (dung) beetle, is an ancient Egyptian symbol of the cycle of life from creation to resurrection.

SEASHELL

The cowrie shell's history as an amulet can be traced back more than 20,000 years, commonly as an evil eye and, secondly, as a fertility symbol. The nautilus is a symbol of perfection. The scallop shell is associated with beauty, romance, and femininity.

SKULL

Among some cultures, such as those of ancient Mexico, likenesses of skulls are amulets that bring good luck and long life, especially if one treats them respectfully.

STAR

Stars stand for truth, guidance, and enlightenment. The classic five-pointed pentagram is a symbol of protection and balance. A hexagram (or Star of David) is the symbol of Judaism and Israel. In antiquity, stars were used as magical signs employed to fend off all forms of misfortune.

SUN

The sun symbolizes eternity, power, hope, and divinity.

T

13

The number 13 has long symbolized fear and death. Both the Chinese and the ancient Egyptians considered the number lucky, interpreting death as a positive transformation into the afterlife.

TOPAZ

The birthstone for November is associated with the Sun. Thought to change color if the food offered the wearer is poisoned, topazes were also used to cure asthma, reverse insomnia, and improve eyesight.

TURTLE

The turtle is a symbol of both heaven (their shell) and earth (their undersides). Turtles also symbolize longevity and immortality.

TULIP

The tulip symbolized perfect love or a declaration of love.

TURQUOISE

The birthstone for December symbolizes prosperity, courage, and success. When given as a gift, turquoise is considered to be a promise of friendship. The most popular of all amuletic stones, it is credited with a wide variety of protective properties.

U

UNICORN

Unicorns represent purity, chivalry, gentleness, and independence.

V

VIOLET

The violet is a symbol of modesty and simplicity.

W

WISHBONE

A wishbone promises good luck when two people make a wish and then pull the sides apart. The one holding the longest piece will have his or her wish come true. If the pieces are of equal length, both contestants are winners.

X

The letter X can represent a sign of anonymity, a stand-in for the Roman numeral 10, or the Greek (as in a fraternity house) letter *Xi* (as in "Theta Xi"). In the context of XOXO (hugs and kisses) it stands for "kisses."

Y

YIN-YANG

The circular black-and-white Yin-Yang symbol represents the union and balance of opposing forces throughout the universe of female yin and male yang.

Z

ZODIAC

The zodiac is the essential symbolic framework of astrology; it takes its name from the Greek word, *zoidiakòs*, meaning "circle of the animals." Every zodiac sign has an associated constellation and figure to represent it.

selected bibliography

Abbott, Mary. *Jewels of Romance and Renown*. London: T. W. Laurie, 1933.

Addison, Josephine, and Diana Winkfield. *Love Potions: A Book of Charms and Omens*. London: Robinson, 1987.

Becker, Vivienne. *Antique and Twentieth-Century Jewelry: A Guide for Collectors*. New York: Van Nostrand Reinhold, c. 1982.

Blum, Dilys E. *Shocking! The Art and Fashion of Elsa Schiaparelli*. Philadelphia: Philadelphia Museum of Art, 2003.

Culme, John, and Nicholas Rayner. *The Jewels of the Duchess of Windsor*. London: Thames & Hudson in association with Sotheby's, 1987.

DeLys, Claudia. *A Treasury of Superstitions*. New York: Gramercy, 1997.

Dubbs Ball, Joanne. *Jewelry of the Stars*. Atglen, PA: Schiffer, 1991.

Ettinger, Roseann. *Popular Jewelry*. Atglen, PA: Schiffer, 2002.

Evans, Joan. *Magical Jewels of the Middle Ages and the Renaissance*. London: Oxford University Press, 1922.

Fales, Martha Gandy. *Jewelry in America 1600–1900*. Woodbridge, England: Antique Collectors Club, 1995.

Flower, Margaret. *Victorian Jewellery*. Mineola, NY: Dover, 2002, an unabridged republication of the work originally published by Cassell, London, in 1951.

Fowler, Marian. *The Way She Looks Tonight: Five Women of Style*. New York: St. Martin's, 1996.

Gibran, Kahlil. *The Prophet*. New York: A. A. Knopf, 1923.

Gill, Brendan, and Jerome Zerbe. *Happy Times*. New York: Harcourt Brace Jovanovich, 1973.

González-Wippler, Migene. *The Complete Book of Amulets & Talismans*. St. Paul, MN: Llewellyn, 1995.

Green, Annette, and Linda Dyett. *Secrets of Aromatic Jewelry*. New York: Flammarion, 1998.

Gregor, Arthur S. *Amulets, Talismans, and Fetishes*. New York: Charles Scribner's Sons, 1975.

Hinks, Peter. *Victorian Jewelry: A Complete Compendium of Over Four Thousand Pieces of Jewelry*, New York: Smithmark, 1991.

Howes, Michael. *Amulets*. New York: St. Martin's, 1975.

Kinross, Patrick Balfour, Lord. *The Windsor Years*. New York: Viking, 1967.

Kunz, George Frederick. *The Magic of Jewels and Charms*. Mineola, New York: Dover, 1997 (an unabridged reprint of the work originally published by J.B. Lippincott, Philadelphia and London, in 1915).

Loring, John. *Tiffany Jewels*. New York: Harry N. Abrams, 1999.

Menkes, Suzy. *The Royal Jewels*. London: Grafton, 1989.

——— . *The Windsor Style*. Topsfield, MA: Salem House, 1988.

Miller, Judith, and John Wainwright. *Costume Jewelry*. London and New York: DK, 2003.

Morris, Desmond. *Body Guards*. Boston: Element Books, 1999.

Mulvagh, Jane. *Costume Jewelry in Vogue*. New York: Thames and Hudson, 1988.

Nadelhoffer, Hans. *Cartier: Jewelers Extraordinary*. New York: Harry N. Abrams, 1984.

Newman, Harold. *An Illustrated Dictionary of Jewelry*. London: Thames and Hudson, 1981.

Papi, Stephano, and Alexandra Rhodes. *Famous Jewelry Collectors*. New York: Harry N. Abrams, 1999.

Percival, MacIver. *Chats on Old Jewellery and Trinkets*. London: T. Fisher Unwin, 1912.

Philips, Clare. *Jewels and Jewelry*. New York: Watson-Guptill, 2000.

Proddow, Penny, and Marion Fasel. *Diamonds: A Century of Spectacular Jewels*. New York: Harry N. Abrams, 1996.

——— and Debra Healy. *American Jewelry: Glamour and Tradition*. New York: Rizzoli, 1987.

——— and Marion Fasel. *Hollywood Jewels*. New York: Harry N. Abrams, 1992.

Rudoe, Judy. *Cartier: 1900–1939*. New York: Harry N. Abrams with The Metropolitan Museum of Art, 1997.

Scarisbrick, Diana. *Jewellery*. London: BT Bratsford, 1984.

Sebold, Alice. *The Lovely Bones*. Boston: Little, Brown, 2002.

Shields, Jody. *All That Glitters*. New York, Rizzoli, 1987.

Slesin, Suzanne. *Over the Top*. New York: Pointed Leaf, 2003.

Smith, H. Clifford. *Jewellery*. New York: G. P. Putnam's, 1908.

Snider, Nick. *Sweetheart Jewelry and Collectibles*. Atglen, PA: Schiffer, 1995.

Snowman, Kenneth A., editor. *The Master Jewelers*. London: Thames & Hudson, 1990.

Taylor, Elizabeth. *Elizabeth Taylor: My Love Affair with Jewelry*. New York: Simon & Schuster, 2002.

Vickers, Hugo. *The Private World of the Duke and Duchess of Windsor*. London: Harrods, 1995.

Woodhead, Lindy. *War Paint: Madame Helena Rubinstein & Miss Elizabeth Arden, Their Lives, Their Times, Their Rivalry*. New York: John Wiley, 2003.

acknowledgments

Both authors would like to say that this book would not have been possible without the vision and commitment of many people at Harry N. Abrams, Publishers, especially: our much-revered editor, Margaret Kaplan; our red-pencil-for-hire, Pam Thomas; Vice-President of art and design, Michael Walsh; our in-book designer, Russell Hassell; our special aide-de-camp, Margaret's assistant, Jon Cipriaso. We also appreciate the efforts of Helen Pratt and the Helen Pratt Literary Agency.

We are forever grateful to those who lent their jewelry, time, and expertise. In alphabetical order, our thanks go to the following:

A La Vieille Russie—Rose Casella and Paul, Peter, and Mark Schaffer; Huma Abedin for Senator Hillary Clinton; Asprey—Lisa Labrado; Letitia Baldrige; Basha; Bergdorf-Goodman—Mallory Andrews; Pedro Boregaard; Cricket Burns; Lisa Caputo; Cartier—Desiré Charles, Nicole Ehrbar, and Olivier Stip; Victoria Casal; Cellini—Michael Graziadei; Chanel—Cécile Goddet-Dirles and Amy Horowitz; C.H.A.R.M.— Leslie and Lisa Slutsky; Charm It! by High IntenCity—Valia; Margaret Chace; Leslie Chin; Chrome Hearts—Della Smith; Liz Claiborne—Margaux Baran; Command PR for Jacob & Co.—Nicole Young; *Daily Fashion Report*—Marilyn Kirshner; Henry Dankner & Sons—Helena Krodel; Jim Davis; Nancy Davis; The Walt Disney Company— Armineh Sarkissian; Hartley du Pont; Emilia Fanjul Communications—Lauren Evans; Ralph Esmerian; Field & Rose—Laura Love Rose; Barberi Paull Feit; Tina Flaherty; Frito-Lay— Jared Doherty and John Hatto; Garrard— Jessica Kim and Seema Mehta; James de Givenchy; Soraya Gomez-Crawford; Lulu Guinness—Leyla Marchetto; Vicki Haberman; Lou Hammond & Associates—Karen Krugel; Elizabeth Herz; Marc Jacobs—Kate Waters;

Jewelry Information Center; Joyce Jonas; Judith Katz-Schwartz; Michael Kaye; Kazuko; Kentshire Galleries—Ellen Israel; Jane Killilea; Neil Lane; Estée Lauder— Evelyn Lauder and Margaret Stewart; Denise LeFrak Calicchio; Lyn Levenberg; Peter Lindeman; Links of London—Jason Paul; Deanna Littell; Elizabeth Locke; Lunch at the Ritz; Chris Madden; Marni; Terry Mayer; The Metropolitan Museum of Art—Stéphane Houy-Towner; Mish—Thea and Ruth Mauro Moncher; Paul Morelli; Odds & Ads—Jack and Pam Coghlan; Helen O'Hagan; Oilily— Sarah; Dr. Mehmet Oz; James Palazza; Philadelphia Museum of Art—Dilys Blum and Carol Platt; Rembrandt— Jennifer Hillman and Susan Wojcik; James Robinson—Joan Boening and Helene Kreniske; Judy Rosenbloom; Chris Royer; Jane Gregory Rubin; St. John—Paula Franco; Lea Seren; Shiseido—Nicole Kardello and Jadzia Tirsh; Suzanne Slesin; Saralee Smithwick; Nick Snider; Sotheby's— Carol Elkins; Stephanie's Antiques; Shelly Stern; Maryanne Strong; Tiffany & Co.— Louisa Bann, Kate Collins, Fernanda K. Gilligan, John Loring, Annemarie Santecki, and Lauren Winer; Trianon (Seaman Schepps)—Colleen Caslin; Van Cleef & Arpels—Christine Drinkard; Verdura— Nicholas and Ward Landrigan, and Christina Payne; Versani—Jonathan Lewis; Louis Vuitton—Aude Mesrie and Iana dos Reis Nunes in Paris, and Jennifer Carlston in New York; Mark Walsh; Cathy Waterman; Stephen Webster—Kate Jarvis and Orlee Winer; June Weir; Wells-Ware—Wells and Pat; White Trash Charms; Harry Winston—Carol Brodie and Carrie Niese; David Yurman—Julie Luchs and John Olsen; Eli Zabar.

FROM JADE—

First I want to thank my charming team—Diny Capland who encouraged me to fasten my seat belt and blast off. Multitalented Marian Walsh, my navigator who explored and conquered beyond the call of duty—her stamina and organizational skills were taken to new heights. I will always be grateful to Brick Ryan—she is my rock, who always seems to amaze me and who hand held me when we hit turbulence—god bless her soul for never losing one piece of jewelry!

During many happy meals to chat and chew—Joseph Montebello at Michaels; my best buddies James Brady and Chris Cerf at Elaine's; my Contessa and play date partner and intermission charm updater at theater, Barbara Plumb at Orso's—lots of pillow talk with cries and whispers with my confidante, Jon Segal.

This book would not have been possible without the cooperation of my shiny stars at Space studio—a profound thanks to Paul Brown for providing his generous services and giving me his diligent staff—and of course we can't pass "Go" without thanking Ona Weatherall for finding solutions to our problematic schedule. My digital guru Schecter Lee—his endless energy and enthusiasm to keep the faith in me—he was our reservoir of fuel—Schecter you are my lucky charm! This book has benefited greatly from the digital skills and expertise of Peter Wong, Dane Shitagi, Alex Beauchesne, and Liz Bailis.

Peter Baiamonte, Robin Riley, and Robyn Lehr—you are my shooting stars making all the precious metal glitter.

My chic charmers—my endless appreciation for your helping hands—inspiring and tweaking the sets and portraits: Matthew Morris and Angela Groff; Rita Madison (Perrella Management); Richard Cooley (Utopia); Irina Krupnik (John Barrett Salon).

FROM KI—

As the writer, I would like to thank: Jeryl Brunner, for your indomitably positive spirit, your creativity, your verbal mastery, and your focus on celebrities; Christy Walker, for your quick study, detailed stickies on the mountain of historical material, plus your expertise on astrology and Eastern religion and culture; John Livingstone, for showing up every day for four months, doggedly getting the details no matter what, and keeping us laughing; Amy Steiner for your dedicated photo research; and Amy Elliott, for your jewelry expertise, your passion for this project, and for working after work almost every night for months to keep the copy flowing.

And words can barely express my gratitude to John Haffner Layden, my editorial anchor, with whom I have worked for many years, for being able to clear his calendar and dig in; for cajoling me out of old writing habits that sprang back into action during this project; and for helping me refine the text.

On the home front, I'd like to thank my husband, Carl Hribar, for his constant support, for keeping himself entertained every night for months, and for reminding me that life will go on. To my wonderful daughters: Caroline Hossenlopp, for locating sources and getting out the initial query letters to hundreds of contacts, and for helping to scour the New York Public Library for important source materials; and Christina Hribar, who input many changes to meet the deadline; and to Caroline's husband, who recently joined our family, Jack Hossenlopp, who gave his love and support at every turn.

index

Page numbers in *italics*
refer to illustrations.

Project Director: Margaret L. Kaplan
Editor: Pamela Thomas
Editorial Assistant: Jon Cipriaso
Designer: Russell Hassell
Production Manager: Justine Keefe

Library of Congress Cataloging-in-Publication Data
Albert, Jade.
The charm of charms / by Jade Albert and Ki Hackney.
    p. cm.
Includes bibliographical references and index.
ISBN 0–8109-5883–x (hardcover : alk. paper)
1. Charms (Ornaments) I. Hackney, Ki. II. Title.
NK4890.C47A38 2005
739.27'8–dc22   2004027043

Photographs copyright © 2005 by Jade Albert

Text copyright © 2005 by Ki Hackney

Printed and bound in China
10 9 8 7 6 5 4 3 2

HNA ▉▉▉▉▉
harry n. abrams, inc.
a subsidiary of La Martinière Groupe
115 West 18th Street
New York, NY 10011
www.hnabooks.com

All photographs in this book are the property
of and are copyrighted by Jade Albert unless
indicated otherwise below. Initial numbers refer
to page numbers.

16: Photograph of Queen Victoria © Hulton-
Deutsch/Corbis
36 (TOP): Photograph of Charm Necklace, Summer
1938, designed by Jean Schlumberger for designer
Elsa Schiaparelli. From the Collection of Leslie Chin.
36 (BOTTOM): Photograph of a diamond bracelet
with nine crosses designed by Cartier and owned
by The Duchess of Windsor. Courtesy of Sotheby's,
Inc. © 1987
81: Photograph of Claudette Colbert, courtesy
of the estate of Claudette Colbert
102: Photograph of President and Mrs. John
F. Kennedy © Bettmann/Corbis
109: Photograph of Louis Vuitton bracelet, courtesy
of Louis Vuitton; Laurent Bremaud, photographer.
140: Photograph of Pearl Bailey © Hulton-
Deutsch/Corbis

Grateful acknowledgment is given for permission
to reproduce the following images in Jade Albert's
photographs:

9: Image of Lucky Charms cereal box. Lucky Charms
is a registered trademark of General Mills. Used with
permission.
48: Image of the paper cut-out couple, courtesy of
Meri Meri Paper Products, Inc. Used with permission.
119: Image of Hulk action figure. Hulk is a registered
trademark of Marvel Characters, Inc. Used with
permission.

Grateful acknowledgment is given to the
following designers and owners for use of
their jewelry for this book. All photographs
are by Jade Albert.

BINDING: Evil-eye jewelry designed by Lea Seren.
FRONT ENDPAPER: A pile of 18-karat gold alphabet
charms designed by Pedro Boregaard.
BACK ENDPAPER: A bracelet of fish, shells, a
Maine lobster, and a diver's mask with a real glass
lens, courtesy of Marilla and Peter Zaremba.
FRONTISPIECE: Over 200 charms on a long gold chain
created and owned by fashion stylist Linda Hopp.
DEDICATION: Albert Albert wearing his "Charmer"
charm collar.
41: Chanel heart necklace, courtesy of Cricket Burns.
105: Chanel belt, courtesy of Vicki Haberman
Vintage Collections.
150–151: Clockwise from far left: Teddy bear,
courtesy of James Robinson Jewelers; Hello Kitty
charm, courtesy of Hello Kitty by Victoria Casal;
fish, courtesy of Margaret Chace; frog, courtesy
of Smithwick Dillon.
152–153: Clockwise from far left, top: lion, courtesy
of Tiffany & Co; owl, courtesy of Anne Phelps; shell,
courtesy of Rembrandt; pearl clover, courtesy of
C.H.A.R.M.; horseshoe, courtesy of Cece Cord.
154–155: Clockwise from far left: sun, courtesy
of Barry Kieselstein-Cord; moveable book,
courtesy of C.H.A.R.M.; turquoise cross, courtesy
of Cricket Burns.
156–157: Clockwise from far left: roulette wheel,
courtesy of Anne Phelps; dagger, courtesy of Cathy
Waterman; polar bear, courtesy of Anne Phelps;
enamel heart, courtesy of Jade Albert.

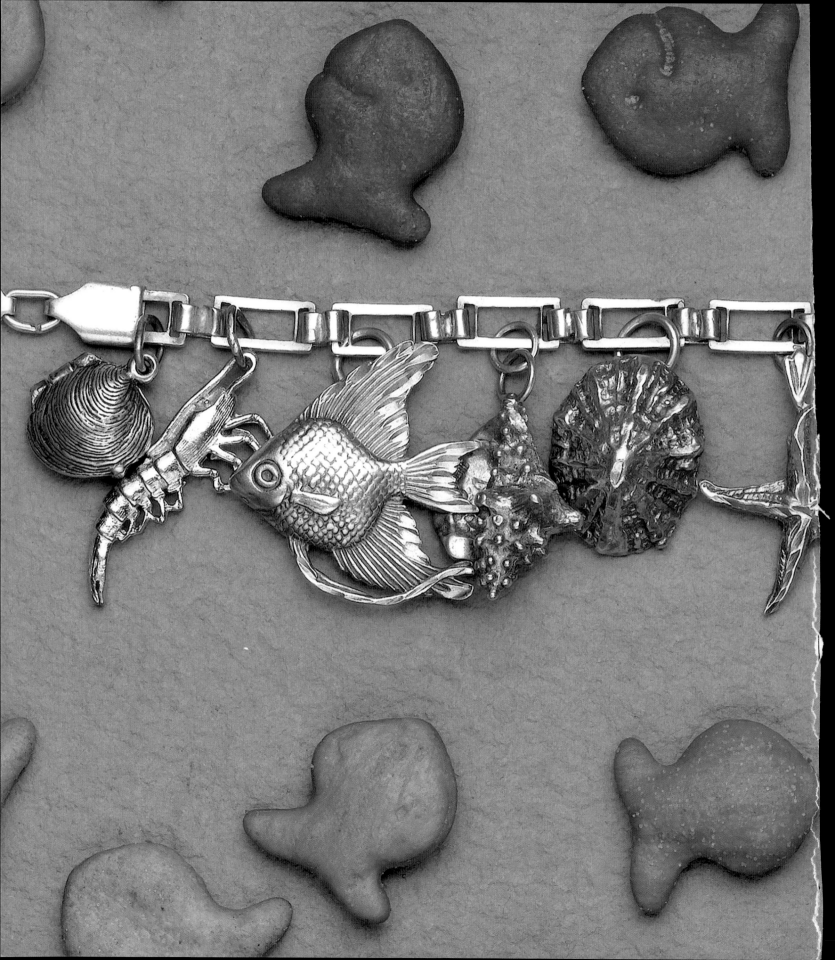